COMMUNITY
BUSINESS

Searching for a Regional Concept

COMMUNITY
BUSINESS

Searching for a Regional Concept

Edited by

SATORU NISHIMURA
MAKOTO HAGINO
ROMEO PEÑA

Border Inc Publishing
Okinawa Prefecture, Japan
www.borderink.com

Design & Lay-out
Paul Serafica
Alondra Sulit
Jo-ann Nishimura

CONTENTS

TABLES

FIGURES

SEARCHING FOR REGIONAL CHARACTERISTICS OF COMMUNITY BUSINESSES

SATORU NISHIMURA

Graduate School of Humanities and Social Sciences
Kagoshima University, Japan

Introduction: Overview of the Activity

Each year Regional Management Research Center and Kagoshima University - Graduate School of Humanities and Social Sciences decide on a regional development-related theme and invite overseas researchers in that field to participate in workshops. The workshops include observations in the relevant fields, status descriptions by local residents and local governments, reports by participants and an exchange of opinions about the observations and reports. For this academic year, the workshop was held over two days from 11th to 12th of January in 2019 at Satsuma-sendai City and Soo City. The invited overseas researchers were Mr. Romeo

Peña from Polytechnic University of the Philippines (Philippines) and Mr. Constantine Busungu from St. Augustine University of Tanzania (Tanzania). The research theme was "Searching for Regional Characteristics of Community Businesses." On the first day of the workshop, a field observation was conducted in Satsumasendai City and an interview survey was conducted in Soo City. On the second day, a reporting meeting and discussion were held. In addition to the overseas guests, the event was attended by members of a domestic research institute, staff from the Satsumasendai City Hall and faculty staff, and graduate students of Kagoshima University (refer to the program at the end of the paper for details).

Positioning the issue: What is a community business?

In this workshop, small business entities that are crucial to the survival of the region and deeply rooted in it are considered to be community businesses. In the mountainous regions and remote islands of Japan, the number of marginal villages is increasing as populations age and birth rates steadily decline. An important task for enabling the continuation of regional economic societies is to identify the kinds of business entities that are necessary for the survival of such villages and clarifying their characteristics. At the same time, in villages in developing countries, identifying the nature of business entities that enable the sustainability of life for people in poverty and understanding the characteristics of such business entities will contribute to resolving the issue of poverty. This workshop aimed to clarify the regional characteristics of regional community businesses by examining cases in Kagoshima, Philippines, and Tanzania.

Observation and Interview Surveys at the Chambers of Commerce: "Barber Street" and Balance of Businesses between Closures and Openings

First, under the guidance of Mr. Takano from Satsumasendai City Hall, we have observed the community businesses in Togocho and Irikicho. Mr. Takano introduced us to several business types: a barbershop and hairdresser, an automobile repair shop, and a liquor shop. We were surprised that these business types maintained a certain number of locations in a small community where aging population and depopulation continue ahead. In particular, one community in Togocho, it was very interesting to see barbershops lined up along one of the main roads. The participants in the workshop named this road "Barber Street."

After that, we visited the Soo City Chamber of Commerce, where we received a briefing with accompanying materials on the number of new business openings and the number of business closings over the six years from fiscal 2013 to fiscal 2018, in each of the three branch offices in Takarabe, Osumi, and Sueyoshi. Then, Mr. Hagino explained the materials. The total number of business closings over the six-year period was 165, significantly outweighing new business openings, which numbered 103 (See Table 1.1). This is to be expected in an area where the industry is waning due to depopulation. However, when examined by industry, the numbers were closer for several business types. These were the 'construction business' and 'the accommodation and restaurant business'. The Chamber of Commerce explained that the construction business in this instance was mainly the housing reform business. It is worth focusing on the fact that these input-output figures were almost in balance. In a limited trade area with little prospect for expansion, it was estimated that these business types experience constant demand (a necessity for residents). In other words, it is much likely that these are community businesses that enable the continuation of the community.

Interview Survey at the Soo City Chamber of Commerce
(Photo by Yusuke Hidaka)

Observation at Barber Street in
Satsumasendai City
(Photo by Yusuke Hidaka)

	Agriculture and forestry	Construction	Manufacturing	Wholesale and retail	Accomodation and restaurant	Life related services and entertainment	Healthcare and welfare	Other	Total
Number of new business openings	7	18	7	25	14	10	7	15	103
Number of business closures	6	22	14	57	14	17	2	33	165
New openings/ closures	1.17	0.82	0.50	0.44	1.00	0.59	3.50	0.45	0.62

Source: Soo City Hall

Table 1.1. Number of Business Openings and Business Closures by Industry in Soo City (Total for Fiscal 2013- Fiscal 2018)

International Comparison of Community Businesses: Kagoshima, Philippines, and Tanzania

Mr. Hagino and Mr. Nishimura started by presenting a report based on economics approaches to the observation of community businesses. Then, Mr. Peña presented a report on small general stores known as *Sari-sari stores* in the Philippines. Lastly, Mr. Busungu presented a report for community businesses in Tanzania.

Mr. Nishimura introduced the Lewis Theory (Lewis 1954) of developmental economics, which explains the mechanism by which the labor force moves from agricultural villages into cities in the transition period of economic development, and noted the importance for regional revitalization of explaining the mechanism for reverse population and labor force movement—from cities to agricultural villages— in Japan today. Mr. Hagino explained the potential for using Chamberlin's theory of monopolistic competition (Chamberlin 1933) in the discussion of community businesses.

A *Sari-sari* store in the Philippines (*From Mr. Peña's report*)

Community businesses in Tanzania (From Mr. Busungu's report)

According to Mr. Peña, the small general stores in the Philippines known as *Sari-sari stores* are an important source of income for people in poverty, that they have a different function from convenience stores such as Seven-Eleven, and that many store owners make a significant contribution to the microeconomy at a grass-roots level despite having a relatively low level of education.

While Mr. Busungu considered community businesses to be businesses that enrich the villages in Tanzania. He introduced several examples of businesses operated by village residents, based on tourism. He went on to emphasize the importance in community business development of retaining a culture that values the village's natural resources and people while making use of them.

Discussion: Is it necessary to consider bazaars as well?

As the discussion progressed, it became clear that the business models that support life are multi-layered in every country, that they differ considerably between the three countries, and that in every country they differ between the cities and the rural areas (See Table 1.2). Based on these facts, the subject for the comparative study of community businesses as businesses that support the daily lives of people in villages became clearer.

Japan		
	Cities	Rural Areas
Main	Medium and large scale modern commercial facilities	
Sub		Small business entities (community businesses)
Philippines		
	Cities	Rural Areas
Main	Bazaars (particularly low-income customers) *Tiangge	
Sub	Small business entities (community businesses) *Sari-sari stores	
Tanzania		
	Cities	Rural Areas
Main	Small business entities (community businesses) *Duka stores	Bazaars
Sub	Bazaars	Small business entities (community businesses) *Duka stores

Table 1.2. Role of community Businesses in Japan, Philippines, and Tanzania

The table shown that in the case of Japan, community businesses could be understood as small business entities that provide supplementary support for daily life to rural residents, while in the Philippines, they were business entities such as *Sari-sari-stores* that provide supplementary support for daily life in cities and rural villages. In Tanzania, small stores similar to *sari-sari stores* are called *Duka*. We found that whereas *Duka* stores are one of the major commercial sectors in the cities, in rural areas they play a supplementary role to bazaars. Moreover, in the Philippines, particularly for low-income earners in cities, a type of bazaar known as *Tiangge* is more important than small general stores such as *Sari-sari stores*. The discussion revealed that in order to understand community businesses that support people's daily lives, it is necessary not only to compare them with modern medium- and large-scale commercial facilities, but also to understand the details of the bazaars.

Future Development: Publishing English-Language Books and English Education Courses

It was confirmed that the workshop result would be published as an English-language book. The planning will be conducted at Kagoshima University, and the editing at the Polytechnic University of the Philippines, to which Mr. Peña belongs. The book is to comprise theories and case studies. The research results of the workshop to date will be used in the Regional Development Course within the MA course in Economic and Social Systems at the Graduate School of Humanities and Economics, Kagoshima University.

During the discussion
(Photo by Yusuke Hidaka)

Workshop participants
(Photo by A staff member of Takarabemori School)

Workshop Program

Project name	Fifth Regional Development International Workshop
	— Searching for Regional Characteristics of Community Businesses —
Date	January 11 (Fri)—12 (Sat), 2019
Venue	Kagoshima University, Satsumasendai City, Soo City
Participants	Guests: Romeo Peña (Polytechnic University of the Philippines)
	Constantine Busungu (St. Augustine University of Tanzania)
	Kagoshima University: Sueo Kuwahara, Makoto Hagino, Yusuke Hidaka, Satoru Nishimura
	Hiroshima Prefecture Osaka Information Center Director: Toru Mochizuki
Schedule	■January 10 (Thursday)
	Arrival of university professors and participants from outside the prefecture at Kagoshima
	■January 11 (Friday)
	○ Community business observation in Satsumasendai City and interview survey at Soo City
	9:00 Depart from the university (bus)
	10:30 Community business observation in Satsumasendai City
	(Guided by City Hall staff)
	12:30 Lunch (Traditional restaurant "Konoan")
	14:00 Travel to Soo City
	16:00 Interview survey at the Soo City Chamber of Commerce
	17:00 Travel to accommodation ("Takarabemori School Hoshi-no-yado)
	18:00 Dinner
	■January 12 (Saturday): Final day, Takarabemori School
	○ Report and Discussion
	9:00 Keynote lectures by Mr. Hagino, Mr. Nishimura, Mr. Peña, Mr. Busungu
	10:30 Group work
	12:00 Lunch (Onsite café)
	13:30 Group work report and summary (Mr. Kuwahara, Mr. Hagino)
	15:00 Publication plan (Mr. Hagino, Mr. Nishimura)
	17:00 Return to Kagoshima City
	■January 13 (Sunday)
	Overseas university faculty staffs depart Kagoshima (return to home countries)

References:

Chamberlin, Edward, 1933. Theory of Monopolistic Competition. Cambridge, MA: Harvard University Press.

Lewis, W. Arthur, 1954. "Economic Development with Unlimited Supplies of Labor," Manchester School of Economic and Social Studies, Vol. 22, pp. 139-91.

REVERSE INTERNAL MIGRATION FROM URBAN TO RURAL IN JAPAN

SATORU NISHIMURA

Faculty of Law, Economics, and Humanities,
Kagoshima University, Japan

Introduction

The aim of the whole book is to clarify the role of community businesses in regional development in different countries. This chapter discusses a broader issue focusing on the Japanese case of Japanese migration. The migration from urban to rural is necessary to tackle the problems of aging and decreasing population in rural areas. Population growth in urban Japan is basically higher than in rural areas at the moment. However, the trend will change under some conditions. This chapter will also describe the emerging change of migration and the reasons behind it. The existence of community businesses is, of course, one of the important factors for a community to become sustainable both economically and socially. It also plays an important role to attract people in urban areas to those in rural areas. The chapter explains other factors by showing an example on a small island in Kagoshima Prefecture in Japan. It also discusses a provisional theoretical approach to grasp the mechanism of migration from urban to rural, which the author names as 'reverse migration' by the several discussion of early development economics.

Internal Migration Trend in Japan

In Japan, people from rural areas are moving into cities to look for employment with higher ages and modern lifestyle. Lewis's model (Lewi 1954) explains the reason behind this movement. The gap in income between rural and urban areas pushed the people from the former to the latter. Figure 2.1 shows the population of immigration to Metro Tokyo and that of emigration from Metro Tokyo. After the Plaza Agreement in 1985 that caused appreciation of Yen and acceleration of the overseas transfer of Japanese companies, many employment opportunities have been lost in urban areas such as Metro Tokyo. The same figure also shows that the number of emigrations increased and that of immigration decreased from 1986 to 1993 in Metro Tokyo. Also, there is an increase in numbers from 2008 to 2011 after the world economic recession caused by Lehman Shock. Besides the two periods, the number of emigrations has been going down, and the number of immigrations has been almost the same. It was only in 1994 when the number of emigrations exceeded that of immigration.

However, if the numbers are examined by age group, a different picture will be seen. Figure 2.2 shows the number of migrations in Metro Tokyo in 2013, it shows that the numbers of immigration exceed a lot in the age group between 18 and 34, but the numbers of immigration and emigration are almost balanced in another age group. It should be noted that the numbers of emigration exceed those of immigration in the age group between 55 to 69. It means that a lot of young people move to Tokyo to study in a high-quality university and to get better jobs. However, there are also a lot of people who exit from metro Tokyo especially among those who are close to the age of retirement.

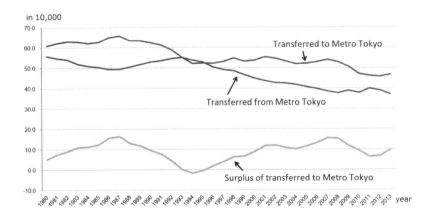

Figure 2.1. Migration trend in Metro Tokyo from 1980-2013
Source: Ministry of Internal Affairs and Communications

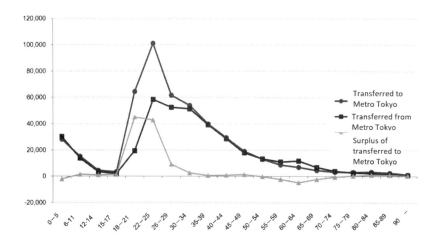

Figure 2.2. Migration in Metro Tokyo by Age Group

There are several reasons why people leave urban areas such as Metro Tokyo. One of them is due to deteriorating infrastructure. According to Mtasutani (2015), some parts of Metro Tokyo will become slums because some of the infrastructures will become out of use. He also says that the area will get a shortage of homes for the aged infrastructures in spite of the accelerating aging population.

Japanese Government Policy for Rural Revitalization: Town/ People/ Jobs

The Japanese government has launched countryside revitalization act (地方再生法) which has been active in tackling the problem of decreasing and aging population in rural areas in Japan. Below is the translation from the web site of the government. Figure 2.3 shows the basic concept of the policy (Japanese Government Policy for Rural Revitalization, 2020).

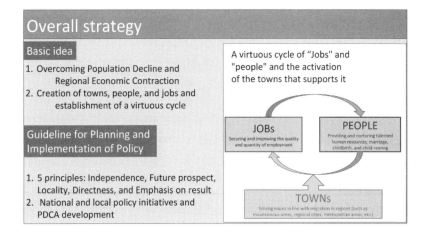

Figure 2.3. Basic guidelines of 'Headquarter for Overcoming Population Decline and Vitalizing Local Economy in Japan
Source: http://www.kantei.go.jp/jp/singi/sousei/mahishi_index.html.

The government will work together to deal with the major challenges facing Japan, such as rapid population decline and super-aging population, and aims to create an autonomous and sustainable society that takes advantage of the characteristics of each region. In order to overcome population decline, secure growth potential in the future, and maintain a vital Japanese society, we are proceeding with policies aimed for these four basic goals: make local work and work with the peace of mind; create a new flow of people to the region; give the younger generations hope for marriage, childbirth, and child-rearing; and last, create a region that fits the time, protect safe living and linking the region with the region.

New Trend of Migration from Big Cities to Rural Areas and Small Islands: Various Patterns

Thanks to government policy and ICT, people are starting to migrate from big cities to rural areas and small islands. According to JOIN (Japan Organization for Internal Migration), the patterns of migration from big cities to the countryside are becoming more diversified.

Figure 2.4 shows the variation of internal migration in Japan. The variation used to be limited to I-turn and U-turn before. I-turn means that people in urban areas go directly to rural areas where they are not from. On the other hand, the U-turn means that the people move back to their hometowns. JOIN also said that there are several newer turns added such as J-turn, X-turn, O-turn, and Z turn. J-turn means that one migrates to the place near his or her home town which has more employment. O-turn means that one moves between an urban area and a rural area regularly after staying at each place for a while. X-turn means that one moves to several remote areas after a while based on a city. One moves several cities and rural areas without having a fixed base in the case Z-turn. Nowadays, people don't necessarily stay in a place to work, even some jobs which relate ICT don't require people to go to an office because people can work at home. Those workers will choose their place and duration of stay in a place more freely than before. The Japanese government policy on work-style reforms will also accelerate the trend. The government is also promoting various styles of work, which help people move to rural areas. Figure 2.5 shows the basic picture of the policy.

Figure 2.4. Various Types of Internal Migration in Japan
Source: Home page of JOIN. https://www.iju-join.jp/feature_cont/guide/003/

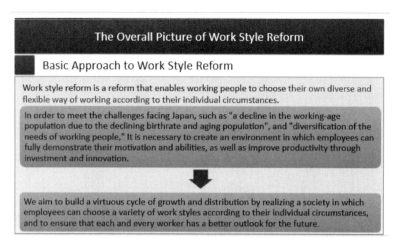

Figure 2.5. Image of 'Work-Style Reforms' by the Japanese Government

Source: Home page of Ministry of Health, Labour and Welfare, https://www.mhlw.go.jp/content/000474499.pdf

A Case of Population Growth in a Small Island

Suwanose Island can be found in Kagoshima Prefecture— which is located in the south of Kagoshima City on Kyushu island (Figure 2.6). Figure 2.7 depicts the transition of the population of Suwanose Island and Toshima Village from 2000 and 2016. The graph indicates that since 2010, the population has kept increasing in the village and Suwanose Island. The population on Suwanose Island increased from 42 in 2010 to 79 in 2016, an increased rate of 88.1%, greatly surpassing the population increase rate of 20% (594 to 713) in Toshima Village during the same period. Figure 8 shows the transition of the population of Suwanose Island by age group in 2002, 2010, and 2016: the youth population (aged less than 15 years), working-age population (15 or older, but under 65 years), and the aged population (65 years and older). The graph shows that the youth and working-age populations have decreased, while the aged population increased between 2000 and 2010. On the other hand, the population of the youth and working-age greatly increased between 2010 and 2016, while the aged population plateaued. The youth population increased greatly from 7 people in 2010 to 24 in 2016. On Suwanose Island, the population increase and the rejuvenation of the population occurred simultaneously.

Moreover, Table 2.1 shows the number of migrants to Suwanose Island, categorizing people who have U/I-turned and the number of I-turning households according to the years from 2009 to 2016. Here, U-turn refers to when people move from the city to another location (in this case, Suwanose Island), then return to their original area of residence. Examining the total for this period, there are 20 U/I-turning households and 15 I-turn households, accounting for 75% of the total number. In terms of the number of people, the former account for 38 and the latter 31, meaning that I-turners account for 81.6% of the total. This shows that I-turners have brought about the population increase/rejuvenation.

Figure 2.6. Location of Suwanose Island (Suwanosejima)

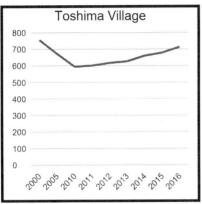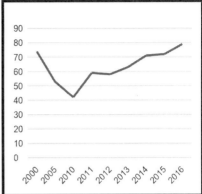

Figure 2.7: Population transition of Toshima Village and Suwanose Island (2000–2016)

Source: Toshima Village Office. Note: Excluding teachers and study abroad students

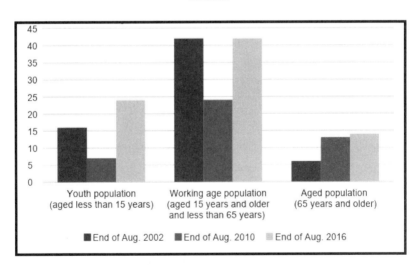

Figure 2.8: Population transition by age group (at the end of August 2002, 2010, and 2016)

Source: Toshima Village Office. Note: Excluding teachers and study abroad students.

	2009	2010	2011	2012	2013	2014	2015	2016	Total (2009-2016)
U/I-Turning Households	1	4	3	1	5	2	1	3	20
Number of U/I-turners	1	6	7	3	11	4	1	5	38
I-Turning Households	1	2	2	0	5	1	1	3	15
Number of I-turners	1	4	6	0	11	3	1	5	31

Table 2.1. Number of U/I-turners and U/I-turning Households in Suwanose Island by Year

Source: Toshima Village Office. Note. Excludes teacher and foreign study students

The major reason Suwanose Island has many I-turners is due to the series of resident settlement promotion policies initiated by Toshima Village in 2010. In 2010, the Village conducted measures such as the Employment Training Bonus Program and the restoration of vacant housing. In 2012, the Resident Settlement Promotion counter of the village office was unified. From 2013, the Village Office started participating in relocation events in urban areas, and in 2014, it secured places of employment. From 2015, it started recruiting volunteers to help in community building activities and opened a nursery. In addition to these policies, the island provides education in small classes and assistance toward childcare expenses.

Mr. A (male, 36 years old), who was interviewed for the purposes of this study, applied for the publicly advertised position of an employee at the Kyudenko Corporation Power Plant located on the island. He was hired, and with his wife and two children, moved to the island seven years ago. While living on the island, he had two more children, so his family currently comprises six members. The reason he decided to relocate to the island was strongly influenced by one factor, namely that he wanted to live in the countryside. However, having a stable job and being able to take time off to raise his children were also important factors. The island has an elementary and middle school, although there are only one to three students per grade, allowing children to receive their education in a small class. In addition, the village grants a monthly child-care allowance of 10,000 JPY (93.90 USD) to the first and second children, and 20,000 JPY (187.80 USD) for the third child onwards. According to Mr. A, unlike Osaka, where they lived previously, he can secure sufficient time to play with his children. He is planning to continue living on Suwanose Island until the youngest child (currently aged two years) graduates from middle school, because of the excellent environment in which to raise children.

The second reason there are many I-turners is the existence of senior I-turners who support the island. Mr. B (male, 72 years old), another respondent for the study, is one of such members. After graduating from university, he embarked on a long trip around the world and then moved to the island aged 26 years to visit Banyan Ashram, a commune on the island that practiced communal living. This commune housed a group referred to as "hippies" by the media, but according to him, it was a "group sustaining themselves to matched human sensibilities through Hinduism or Buddhism." The commune started when Suwanose elders begged Nanao Sakaki, who was visiting the island, to bring more young people there to live at the onset of the population decline. This was consequent to the island having to close, because of a lack of young people to perform boat-related jobs such as loading and unloading shipments. He belonged to a group called Buzoku in Japan, but contacted his peers and created a commune in 1967 along with members such as the American poet Gary Snyder. Many young people visited the commune and collaborative living had commenced by 1977/1978. Thereafter, many members of the commune left the island, but some remained and lived in a household unit. Those who remained became island residents and supported the island by participating in its activities and events. Currently, five households play a central role in running various events as the elders of the island. Events include festivals held by the shrine and those run by the residents' association and schools. Events held at the shrine include the fishing festival (January and May), ship-launching festival (January), O-bon Lantern Festival (August), and festival for praying (October). While the events held by the residents' association include road repair (July and December), Bon dance (August), Arasetu and Shibasashi dances (September and October) that originated in the Amami-Shoto Islands, and welcoming and farewell parties for transferring members (April and March). School events are also important activities in which children and adults participate, including the athletics meeting (September), cultural festival (November), and long-distance relay race (January). As seen, events on Suwanose Island seamlessly take place throughout the year. Senior I-turners serve as the organizers of this series of events.

Month	Date	Residents' association events	School events	Notes
4	6	New transfer welcoming party	Entrance ceremony	
	26	General Residents' Association Assembly		
5	31			Fishing festival
7	1	Roads repair (cleaning activity)		
	2	"		
8	13	Bon dance for welcoming		Lantern Festival (Bon Festival)
	15	Bon dance for parting		"
	16			Mountain festival
	29	Summer festival		
9	16		Athletic meets	
	25	Arasetsu Dance		
	26	"		
10	1	Shibasashi Dance		
	2	"		
	4	Full moon night		
	8	Old water resource cleaning task		
	14			Festival for praying
11	4		Cultural festival	
12	2	Roads repair (cleaning activity)		
	7		Long distance relay race	
1	1	New Year's celebration		
	2			Boat celebration (ship owners)
	11			Fishing festival
	14			Nari mochi
2	23		Farewell excursion trip	
3	10		Graduation ceremony	
	Undecided	Transfer farewell party		

Table 2.2. 2018 Residents' Association Events
(Suwanose Island)
Source: Suwanose island Resident's Association

Although Suwanose Island still has various tasks to tackle in the future, like the lack of vacant housing and settlement of I-turners after their allowance has been cut, but still, the present vitalization of the island via I-turners has been successful. The factors for this success are explained by the following two points from the perspective of "diversity." The first is the diversity of the island residents. The island became isolated after a major volcanic eruption in 1813, with Tomiden Fujii from the Amami-shoto Islands settling 70 years later in the 1880s. Thereafter, the establishment of a commune in the late 1960s formed the island residents' group mentioned earlier. The descendants of the settlers from Amami-shoto islands and island residents from the commune overcame their differences and created a community. This is believed to have created a culture that approved of I-turners, who have diverse values. The second factor is the collaborative relationship between various organizational bodies. Island residents work towards receiving I-turners by collaborating with the village office and NPOs. An NPO organization, namely Takara Interface, also plans and runs island visit tours for those wishing to I-turn.

The results of interviews with Mr. A and Mr. B revealed important points regarding the future prospects of the island. From a financial efficiency viewpoint, it is difficult for public or private institutions to provide higher education and advanced medical treatment based on the population size of Suwanose Island. As such, once the children graduate middle school, they must leave the island to advance to high school. There is the option of the parents staying on the island until the youngest of their children graduates from middle school, for which primary education is subsidized, and send an allowance to their children living outside the island, as Mr. A is planning to do. However, many people likely leave the island as a family when their oldest child advances to high school. Furthermore, as they age, many people like Mr. B will be forced to move to an urban area equipped with advanced medical institutions to receive medical treatment for their spouse or themselves. In other words, the discrepancy in education and medical service between the island and the city creates a structure that generates a certain percentage of people regularly emigrating from the island. Therefore, more people moving to the island than those leaving are needed. To do so, it is necessary to enhance and provide support for primary education, and to create industries that are high in productivity and can make a good living, both of which are currently possible in Toshima Village. This will probably center on the agriculture and fishery as well as tourism industries.

Moreover, public relations for the islands must be conducted by hosting events in the cities to promote resident settlement. An island that has many people leaving and many moving in at the same time will signify that the island residents will have diverse ways of thinking, leading to a strong likelihood of creating a flexible and vital economy and society. In addition, information on vacant housing and the repair thereof must be available to attract settlers. Toshima Village effectively executed such policies and activities. Table 2.3 summarizes the various activities implemented by Toshima Village to promote   residents' settlement in the village (Toshima Village, 2017). The chart indicates the Employment Training Bonus   Program as the basis for the creation of the industry. Public relations events are vigorously conducted in the local   Kagoshima Prefecture, Kanto region, and urban regions, with the smooth renovation of vacant housing and provision thereof to new migrants. However, as mentioned, the lack of vacant housing may become an obstacle in accepting migrants in the future.

	Major policies/activities	Notes
2010	**The Employment Training Bonus Program (which serves as the basis of the relocation policy) is initiated.** The vacant housing usage program is started.	By 2016, 24 vacant houses are prepared.
2011	Briefing seminars are hosted locally.	
2012	Community Promotion Section is newly established (Resident Settlement Promotion counter unified into one counter) The Settlement Project Team is launched. * Comprises each island's residents' association chief, local politicians, and dispatched agents	
2013	Participated in a relocation event in urban areas.	
2014	The Site Operations Work Program is started. A solo event is held in Tokyo.	
2015	Recruitment of volunteers to participate in community building activities begins. Conferences on the Settlement Project are held on all islands.	According to the national census, Suwanose Island ranks second in Japan in terms of the population increase rate by municipality.
2016	The two volunteers for community building activities (stockbreeding assistants) start their activities. Event held only by the Village is held in Tokyo.	

Table 2.3. Resident settlement policies in Toshima Village

Source: Created based on Toshima Village (2017) Takara Islands; full of fascinating Islands < Resource Edition>

Community Business as a Condition for Reverse Migration

In the case of Suwanose Island, the government policy to create employment has greatly contributed to the population growth. However, there are several conditions which enable the rural areas to become sustainable both economically and socially. One condition is the existence of community business (CB). CBs create jobs, people who cherish the community and eventually build a sustainable town. A CB in a rural area has a different economic mechanism from the big businesses in urban areas. One of the most important differences between the two businesses is that a CB do not necessarily seek to make the average profit rate in the urban areas. If a community business can create benefits in the community, the benefit will be distributed to the owner of the community.

Thus, if the owner of the CB totals the actual profit and the communal benefit per person, the amount may exceed the average profit. And there may be some mechanism for a CB to attract customers. In the case of 'barber street', there seem to be more shops than demand considering the population there. There may be a unique mechanism working. The discussion and answers should be left to Mr. Takano. If we define a *Sari-sari* store as a CB, the barbershop and *Sari-sari* store have some similarities. One is that the customers live in or near the community where the CB is located. The customers can walk to the CB to do shopping or receive a service. The owner and the customers are so close to talk about what is going on in the community. The relationship can make the community tie stronger. Especially in the case of the rural communities in Japan where the aged and decreasing population is going on, it is crucial to issue to prepare enough labor to carry on community works such as cleaning the streets, organizing sports festivals and so on. A strong tie in the community also serves to keep an eye on the safety of old people, especially those who live alone.

One of the effective ways to make a CB sustainable is to use the natural resources in the community to lessen the running cost. Our research group in Kagoshima University once collaborated on a social experiment in Kirishima City, Kagoshima with the people in the community. Regional Development Research Center of Kagoshima University panned the project and got permission to carry on the project by the community (See 'A Community Business project by Regional Development Research Center') The researchers put a long pipe in the river which is elevated and suitable for the machine to operate, and installed a small scale hydro energy generator down to the village side. We built a power charging station to make a tiny electric car to be charged. We rent 'Toyota COMS' (Figure 2.9) for the   project. Arranged it so that the shop which sells mainly   local products named 'Kirakukan' could charge the car at the station and an employee can drive around the   community to deliver the goods on demand. The car was named as 'Kiraku Go'. A villager helped us make a sticker for the car. A shopkeeper lady made a nice brochure to promote the project in the community. The merits of the project are not only to lessen the running cost by not using fuel but also to watch the situation of the old people,   especially living around in the time of delivery.

Many of the old people in the community are old enough to walk to a shop and stay in their house for a whole day. The project made an elderly customer possible to buy the local foods by just calling the shop and have time to have a chat with a driver who was a neighbor even just for a while. People in the community really liked the project and 'Kiraku Go', or a small EV car became an 'idle' in the community. An unexpected positive cycle started. The employees in the municipality ordered the shop to deliver 'bento' or lunch boxes. Many *Bentos* were also ordered during community events such as 'undo-kai', or a sports festival. The fact shows that once a project is considered as a part of the community, people will voluntarily get involved in it. It can be said that the project of hydro energy was accepted and became a kind of CB.

There are several reasons why the university project went smoothly. First, there was a strong supporter of the project in the community. It was a retired professor from Kagoshima University, Mr. Masaharu Manda. He is now engaged in organic rice farming using ducks instead of chemical insecticides. He also organizes farming school regularly. Thanks to him, several young couples moved to the community to do organic farming, which helped the community to be vitalized. When we had a meeting for the first time with people in the community, several attendants were dubious over the plan— thinking that the university was bringing something. Mr. Manda was patient enough to help us defend a series of questions some of which are offensive. There is a discussion that a Resident Innovator plays an important role when an innovative community development project is introduced in a community. He is the one to translate what is all about the project using simple terms and taking enough time until other members understand. He should be responsible for what will happen after the project starts, otherwise, he or she will be blamed in the community.

Figure 2.9. Toyota COMS, Kiraku Go

After the project, our team left the community and asked the people if they would like to continue the project. We promised them that they could use the power generating machine until they don't need it. The small electric vehicle was bought by Mr. Manda. After a while, they stopped using the power facility because the charging station was a bit far from the shop and the road was rough. But Mr. Manda still continues to maintain the facility and planning to use it for charging electric fences to prevent the wild animals from getting near towards the farms. The delivery service by an electric vehicle is still going on even though the car is being charged by the plague in the shop. One thing that we should note is that all the equipment and other running costs of the project were prepared by the university. The project is customized by the people and is continuing, but the cost paid by a person was indispensable. If the government or the local government such as prefecture and municipalities support the community in cash or kind, the project may become more successful than otherwise.

Economic Theory to Approach the Issue of Migration from Urban to Rural

As explained above, people will move from urban to rural under some conditions. If the social and economic mechanism or system of the migration, government, local government, Non-Profit Organization (NPO) are able to know what they should and how much cost they should prepare.

The author considers that the discussion of a dual economy that started way back in the 1950s to 1970s by several eminent development economists such as Sir William Arthur Lewis. His economic development theory is based on the dual economy of an urban sector under the industrialization and rural sector under a limited supply of labor (Lewis 1954). He points out that the wage level in the rural area is so low at subsistence level because the production level is quite low in the rural areas. Then the capitalists can hire the workers in the rural areas for their industrial production at an extremely low level. Thus, migration of the rural people leads 'rosy' economic development thanks to low wages in urban areas which makes the profit bigger than otherwise. The work of Fei and Ranis (1970) discusses the point when the migration starts. According to them, migration will end when the shortage of labor in the rural areas increases the wage to the level of that in urban. Harris and Todaro's (1970) analyze how rural people decide to migrate to the urban. The discussion of growing 'informal sector' is also helpful in understanding the reverse migration. In the discussion, the informal sector in urban is considered as a sector where the migrated people collect information on the formal sector and they adjust themselves to urban life. It is important that the urban economy itself is considered to be dual. This dualism is actually happening in big cities such as Tokyo and Osaka in Japan. There are people with high incomes and those with low incomes. The patterns of reserve migration differ between the two groups. The upper class who doesn't need to stick to a single workplace will migrate to rural searching for extra benefits while living there. On the other hand, the lower class whose wage level is almost the same or less seek for the job in rural and extra benefits.

It explains that the rural people calculate the expected lifetime income between the hometown and the urban area to head for if the former is bigger, he or she makes the action. Otherwise, he or she stays where he or she lives.

These discussions point out dual economy, turning point and decision-making process of the migrants from economic viewpoints. The merging of the approaches is possible in understanding the process of migration from urban to rural in Japan and other countries of the same situation. Firstly, it can be said that the rural economy and the urban economy in Japan are very different. It is very difficult to get the average profit in rural areas. But the situation which differs from that of developing countries is that there is no affluent labor and the population is decreasing and aging on the contrary. It is necessary to come up with a new theory of a dual economy in Japan. Second, the discussion of the turning point also needs to be modified to clarify why people in Japan migrate from urban to rural. One assumption is the accelerating dual economy in urban areas. The income gap between rich and poor is increasing there, so the gap of income between rural and urban shrink if only the low-income class dwellers in urban are focused. The second assumption is that some people don't need to choose the place to stay thanks to ICT, and considering the benefit of a healthy life surrounded by nature and good education in some areas. The mutual helping system in some rural areas is considered to be benefits for the migrant. There is a social problem especially in urban areas called 'lone death' in Japan. In some rural areas, there are still strong community ties going on which help 'the excluded people from the society'. It should be noted that it is not always the case in rural areas.

Even in the theory of Lewis, rural people can automatically migrate and help industrialize the country or a region. The rural people need to be educated enough to be employed in a modern economic sector. People in urban areas can calculate the expected income and additional benefits in the rural area to migrate for a certain period of time, and if it is bigger than staying in the urban area where they live. Basically, the turning point is up to the individual, but there could be several groups depending on the age, job, and other attributes.

Conclusion

Migration in japan is basically happening from rural to urban at the moment. However, the trend may change after the infrastructure in urban areas become old and the income gap grows. ICT is enabling the people to work in rural areas and the people in rural areas can buy almost all which those in urban are buying by using online shopping. On the contrary, the positive features such as the richness of culture, community ties, and rather inexpensive education cost are attracting the attention of the people from urban areas. It is not easy but it is possible to make a model of the 'reverse migration' by borrowing the classic development theories.

Another important thing is that the economy in urban now in Japan is dual between urban and rural. And the urban economy is also a dual, or high-income economy and low-income economy. In the development economic theory, the dual economic sectors in the urban, or formal and informal sector are considered to be closely connected. In a simple way, the informal sector is considered a steeping sector to the formal. In the present Japanese economy, the two groups should be considered as divided. Thus, the mechanism of the migration with high income should be considered in different ways.

References:

A Community Business Project by Regional Development Research Center—Kagoshima University. Retrieved from https://www.youtube.com/watch?v=DUtID62 HyG8. (Accessed on March 9, 2020).

Fei, J.C.H. and Ranis, G. (1961) A Theory of Economic Development. The American Economic Review, 51, 533-565.

Harris, John R. & Todaro, Michael P. (1970) Migration, Unemployment, and Development: A Two-Sector Analysis", American Economic Review, 60 (1): 126–142.

Japanese Government Policy for Rural Revitalization. Retrieved from http://www.kantei.go.jp/jp/singi/sousei/mahishi_index.html. (Accessed on March 9, 2020).

Kagoshima Prefecture (2014). Information Magazine for Those Who Wish to Settle in Toshima Village.

Lewis, W. Arthur (1954). Economic Development with Unlimited Supplies of Labour. The Manchester School. 22 (2): 139–91.

Resident Retirement Management Office, Community Promotion Section, Toshima Village.

Suwanosejima Elementary and Junior High School Homepage. Retrieved from http://www.toshima-sc.net/suwanose/ (Accessed on March 9,2020).

Toshima Village (2017). Takara Islands; full of fascinating islands <Resource Edition>, TRY-SHA, Co., Ltd.

Toshima Village Official Homepage. Retrieved from http://www.tokara.jp/ (Accessed on March 9, 2020).

Acknowledgment:

I would like to extend my gratitude to Mr. Manda in Kirishima city, Mr. Kumamoto from the Toshima Village Office, Mr. Ito, a Village Office branch member, and the people from the Island for cooperating in the research and investigation conducted to write this paper.

ON THE TRANSFORMATION OF COMMERCIAL AGGLOMERATION IN DEPOPULATED AREAS AND NEW ECONOMIC CIRCULATION: A COMPARATIVE STUDY OF THE CASE OF HIROSHIMA PREFECTURE WITH THE CASE OF KAGOSHIMA PREFECTURE

TORU MOCHIZUKI

Osaka office of Hiroshima Prefectural Government

Changes in Commercial Agglomeration in Depopulated Areas and New Economic Circulation

Summary of the Survey Results of Hiroshima Case

Based on the theory of (1) entry/exit circulation and (2) high charge level of acceptance conditions of establishment of community business pointed out by Takano (2016) in Kagoshima, the existence of similar phenomenon which is the depopulation area in Hiroshima Pref., a comparative analysis was conducted for Akiota-cho, Osaki-kamijima-cho, Sera-cho, and Jinseki-kogen-cho and additionally administered a field surveys for Sera-cho and Jinseki-kogen-cho were further detailed

41

in this paper.

First, let's briefly take a look at the outline of Christaller's central place theory that Takano relies on. Walter Christaller is a German geographer who has analyzed the characteristics of the distribution of goods and services in the region and established the central place theory (Christaller, 1933). Christaller conceptualized "that central places would facilitate efficiency through the development of a small number of higher-order centers (large cities) and a larger number of lower-order centers (smaller cities and towns). Higher-order centers are places where higher-order goods (high-priced items purchased infrequently, such as cars or jewelry) are traded, whereas lower-order centers are more easily accessed through reduced travel costs, and serve as places where lower-order goods (low-priced items purchased frequently, such as milks or eggs) are traded" (Aoyama, Murphy & Hanson 2011, p.209).

As shown in Figure 3.1, the central place theory consists of three principles: the supply principle (= K3 system), the traffic principle (= K4 system), and the administrative principle (= K7 system). The Christaller's supply principle (= K3 system) is a central system based on a homogeneous plane, which is based on a primary means of transportation such as walking or wagons. Christaller also presented the traffic principle (= K4 system), and the administrative principle (= K7 system), based on the supply principle (= K3 system). The traffic principle (= K4 system) shows the change of the central location system by a straight traffic route such as the construction of a railway. On the other hand, the administrative principle (= K7 system) assumes that steep mountains and rivers are located on the central ground. These principles indicate that the number and distribution of centers vary depending on the historical background, natural environment, and under what political system they were formed (Matsubara 2013, pp.43-44).

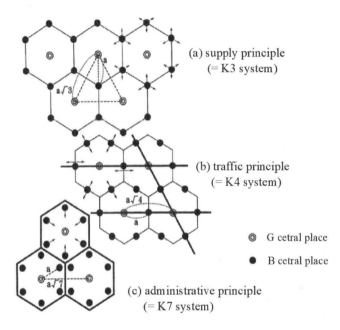

Figure 3.1 Three Principles of Christellar's Central Place Theory
Source: Matsubara, 2013, pp. 43

Next, let's look at an overview of the survey results in Hiroshima Prefecture. In the first results in the case of Hiroshima Pref., the emerging phenomenon of the community business that Takano (2016) shows could not be confirmed. Rather, among the three environmental factors that surround Christaller's central place theory namely the transformation of consumer behavior, the strategic location of the commercial capital, and the information and communications revolution, among others, the influence of the strategic location of the commercial capital appears strongly in any city. From this, it was confirmed that the uniform distribution of shops based on the supply principle of Christaller was almost collapsed and largely deformed.

Second, a trend was confirmed to compensate for the straw phenomenon that accompanies commercial accumulation in the central area due to the strategic location of commercial capital. Specifically, the establishment of Tsuna shop by designated management in Sera-cho and the movement of mobile sales of Tanabe Shoten (grocery shop) appeared as a complement to the traffic principle (= K4 system) in consumer behavior. As for complementation by mobile sales, it was also confirmed in Jinseki-kogen-cho.

Thirdly, taking into consideration the possibility of downsizing public buses after three years of social experiments, Jinseki-kogen-cho has introduced a system of low-priced, free-run taxis that are rare in Japan. This is a measure that goes beyond the demand-type shared bus and private paid service, which are the mainstream. This Jinseki Fureai Taxi has emerged as a modern solution to the administrative principle (= K7 system) in consumer behavior.

In this way, the consumer behavior, the strategic location of commercial capital, and the information and communication revolution are multiplied by the supply principle (= K3 system), the traffic principle (= K4 system), and the administration principle (= K7 system). By analyzing together, it was possible to consider the relationship of consumer behavior to the traffic principle (= K4 system) and administrative principle (= K7 system). At the same time, this analysis framework also provides a framework that considers Takano's model as a complement to the supply principle (= K3 system) in consumer behavior. And, the emergence of community business in the sparsely populated area of Takano (2016), together with its inverse Lewis characteristics[1], was able to be read as a signal that tells another economy's sign, according to this Hiroshima Pref.'s survey. If the third environmental factor 'information and communication revolution' is replaced with the 'new trend of the age' representation and the application is extensible, it represents the new signal of the target area of Hiroshima Pref. which is another thing that can be analyzed together with the signs of solidarity economy and community economy. To reiterate, there are three main principles of Christaller: supply principle (= K3 system), traffic principle (= K4 system), and administrative principle (= K7 system). On the other hand, there are three changes in the environment surrounding the region: the transformation of consumer behavior, the strategic location of commercial capital, and the information and communication revolution. The purpose of this paper was to clarify how these three principles relate to three environmental factors, beyond a simple comparison with Takano (2016). And the above considerations are the consequences of such awareness. As a result, with regard to the state of the commercial facilities surrounding the depopulated area, not only is the task ahead of the crisis that is now more seized, more clearly and sharply but also the possibility of the community business was confirmed. In particular, the fifth property is an important issue that illustrates the extensibility of the inverse Lewis theory, so I will explain it in the next section as a sprout of another economy.

Influence of Strategic Location of Commercial Capital in Depopulated Area of Hiroshima Prefecture

As we have seen so far, the influence of the strategic location of commercial capital appears in the environment surrounding the depopulated area of Hiroshima Pref. In addition, there is an infrastructure factor called the development of the wide area expressway network in the background. Hiroshima Pref. has relocated Hiroshima Airport from Hiroshima City in the western part of Hiroshima Prefecture to Mihara City in the central part, achieving one-hour airport access from any region in Hiroshima Pref. But in addition to the opening of Chugoku-zyukan do and Sanyo do, Onomichi and Matsue do (High-speed express national highway) opened in 2015, starting from Onomichi city in Hiroshima Pref. It is 137 km extending to Matsue city in Shimane Prefecture on Japan sea via Miyoshi city in the north and the Onomichi-Matsue access time was shortened from 2 hours and 30 minutes to 1 hour and 20 minutes, which conventionally took 3 hours and 50 minutes. As a result, the high-speed transportation network that had been concentrated in the western part of Hiroshima Pref. has been improved, and a well-balanced transportation network has been completed in the east, west, north, and south. In other words, by adding the eastern southern axis of Onomichi and Matsue-do to Hamada do, which is the north-south axis of the existing west, a well-gone network with good balance has been completed.

With the opening of Hamada do, ALPark, a complex shopping center in Nishi-ku, Hiroshima City, not only incorporated Akiota-cho into the sphere of influence in the Hiroshima metropolitan area but also attracted customers from San-in, mainly in Hamada City. In addition, there was a major supermarket opening in Osaki-kamijima-cho, and even in the islands, there was a competition over the share of Hiroshima-based supermarkets, Izumi and Fresta. Furthermore, the commercial concentration of Route 432 on the roadside attracted nearly twice as many users as the actual population of Sera-cho. The Sanwa area in the south is under the influence of Fukuyama City, and even in Jinseki-Kogen-cho, which does not receive any benefits from the development of the expressway network, has a strong influence on commercial accumulation such as Fuji Gran in the north region (Kanabe) of Fukuyama City. Unlike Hiroshima City in Akiota-cho, and Higashi-hiroshima City in Osaki-kamijima-cho, Sera-cho and Jinseki-kogencho-cho have less susceptible to highways and conversely geographical to commercial accumulation in neighboring cities and towns. The widening of the area due to the merger of municipalities has spurred this. In particular, the commercial area of the Jinseki-kogen-cho was divided, under the influence of the neighboring commercial area.

Among them, the uniform distribution in the central place theory of Christaller that Takano (2016) showed was almost collapsed in Sera-cho and Jinseki-kogen-cho, except for some areas like Toyomatsu-son. In the case of Sera-cho, the conversion of straw around the roadside commercial facilities on Route 432 is a major factor. While in Jinseki-kogen-cho, the topographic vulnerability that was originally contained is more pronounced due to the declining birthrate, aging and declining population after the municipal merger during the Heisei era. On the other hand, the Fureai taxi policy (described later, K7 = administrative principle) taken by Jinseki-kogen-cho was an excellent measure, although there was an urgent need. However, it has not been possible to elucidate why the former Toyomatsu-son, whose population has been halved at peak time, can maintain the uniform distribution of the central place theory of Christaller. It was thought that Takano (2016) points out that the resident's temperament, which accepts high rates, reflects this. However, in this survey, it was impossible to consider the residents' consciousness.

Complementing the Traffic Principle (=K4 System) in Consumer Behavior

The frequent occurrence of traffic accidents by elderly drivers in urban areas has become a severe social problem in Japan, and the return of driver licenses for elderly people is recommended. On the other hand, the return of a driver's license did make elderly people difficult to travel is a serious problem in depopulated areas where cars are the indispensable means of transportation.

The Tsuna Shop, where the service began in the northwestern region of Sera-cho, is also aimed at helping elderly people who cannot drive these cars. This is because the nearest commercial facilities (located in the center of Miyoshi City and Sera-cho) is 15km away from here. With the opening of the shop, local residents have access to daily necessities within walking distance. In addition, since the Miyoshi-Chuo-hospital in the adjacent area of the Miyoshi City is a little closer in distance than the Sera-cho-hospital in Sera town, the traffic of the demand-type shared taxi service (600 yen/once) eliminated this inconvenience. In the Sera West area, the Sera West Town Center, as the gateway to the city (the easternmost end), was established and the functions of the old town were concentrated in the small country at the eastern end of the town. The only supermarket in this area called Komeri (sole supermarket in formerly Sera Nishi-cho) was also located at this far east end. The Tsuna shop and the shared taxi were also corrections of this distortion.

In addition, the East District's Self-Government Association (827 people/331 households) runs an accommodation facility (Sera-no-yado Higashi) using closed school. This facility is used for overnight nursery schools and school camps. Throughout the stay, the maximization of elementary school as an educational facility for increasing interaction between visitors and the community was made through activities such as konjac making and kimuchi making. It is difficult for housewives in the area where child care has been settled down to spend time on facility services because they already have other jobs. The facilities are having difficulty finding workers. However, the return is a serious problem for the region, due to the high dependence on cars. This is why the local grocery store "Tabuchi Shoten" has started mobile sales and is supporting these shopping refugees. In response to requests from residents, "Tabuchi Shoten" has expanded its service to the Io Self-Government Center. Tsuna shop and Tabuchi Shoten's mobile sales is an indispensable service for those who can't enjoy the benefits of the commercial accumulation on Route 432 bypass. But from now on, as the number of the returnees of driver's licenses over the age of 80 increases, it can be seen that this is a common problem not only in Sera-cho, but also in county areas where cars are essential in daily life and that it is an appropriate solution nationally. Thus, this factor complements the behavior of consumers who are inaccessible with the benefits in the motorization with traffic principle(=K4 system).

Today's Solution to the Administrative Principle (=K7 System) in Consumer Behavior

Sanwa-cho, located in the center of Jinseki-Kogen-cho, was under the influence of Fukuyama City before the merger of municipalities, but the relationship with Fukuyama City further deepened due to the construction of housing complexes after the merger. In addition, the Jinseki area is drawn in three directions, such as Tojo, Shobara, Joge, and Sera, and the residents go out for shopping in their vicinity. Mobile sales are in a situation to complement it. On the other hand, in the Yuki area, the Ono district in the north is drawn to Tojo and the Senyogahara in the south is drawn to the Kanabe and although there are high school, bank, agricultural cooperative (JA), and other base facilities, a lot of shops in the center of Yuki were closed.

Lawson opened the 'Yamabiko Lawson Jinseki kogencho store' in August 2011 at the request of Jinseki kogencho along Route 182 and the sales output was stable at about 140 million yen annually. A company with a capital of Fuchu City (Joge) had opened two 30m² supermarkets named Tulip in Jinseki-kogen-cho (Yuki, Sanwa), but the Yuki store closed about 10 years ago and the Sanwa store also closed in 2018. The latter is the business successor of Flex (Onomichi capital). In that sense, Lawson covers this. However, the fact that sales of about 140 million yen also talks about that Lawson was like a double face of Janus who hollowed out the store in the center of Yuki while giving convenience to the city.

In addition, Lawson introduced a special car 'Lawson' for minicars from March 2012 and is conducting mobile sales and order delivery for those who have difficulty coming to the store. Sales of "Lawson" is about 1 million yen a year, may seem to be small but it responds to the needs of the desired self-government promotion area (2 districts in the Jinseki area e.g. Kusaki and Ikugawa and 1 district in Toyomatu area e.g. Nisaka). Also, Konishi Shoten (food and liquor stores) and Nakahira Shoten (food, sundries, liquor, and tobacco) in Toyomatsu also support difficult areas with mobile sales. However, although the contribution of these stores to the area is high, as estimated from the sales of Lawson, the amount is very small. This can be considered as the background behind 'Jinseki Fureai Taxi' that can be freely used at a fixed flat rate at once that is beyond the demand-type shared bus and private paid service.

However, as we saw earlier, firstly, registered residents were freed from route and time constraints and were free to go to hospital, shop and eat. Second, 1,680 people, approximately 90% of the 2,610 target people (qualified people), are registered, and a total of 43,500 people use them as valuable transportation. This amount of public transport expenditure also has created a new economic circulation of 110 million yen in this region. This can be said to be a kind of effective demand policy or a key policy of relegation. Even in the country, it is rare to find a way to open taxis without restrictions. This is a combined measure that creates effective demand and regional economic circulation based on the regional characteristics of the town, as well as being a reduction model in the population decline phase. Jinseki Fureai taxi for elderly people has significance as a solution to the administrative principle (= K7 system) in consumer behavior.

Takano's Model as a Complement to the Supply Principle (=K3 System) in Consumer Behavior

In this part, community business as a new economic circulation in the area presented by Takano (2016) and in terms of consumer behavior is the supply principle of Christaller's central place theory. It turns out that it is one of the solutions of distortion correction in the relation between (= K3 system) and consumer behavior. A new company enters the store where it was empty and circulates. Even if you go out of business, there is a metabolism that someone enters. Blank shops such as a barbershop, an automobile maintenance factory, and a construction shop will be filled. Although this economic cycle, based on Chamberlain's theory of exclusive competition, could not be confirmed in this survey in the Hiroshima Pref., these companies are eliminating the distortions between consumer behavior and supply principles through community businesses that solve regional issues. It is driven by the fulfillment of social responsibility to maintain the community.

This community business model is versatile because of its fundamental nature of reciprocity. In addition, as a theory that connects the supply principle of this centralist theory with "transformation of consumer behavior", it can be applied to areas with the same geographical background as Satsuma-sendai city. This approach also provides an important perspective from the inverse Lewis Theory to the other economy, as seen in the next chapter. This is a useful research result for which further theoretical evolution is desired, such as improving the generalization requirements by refining the establishment and survival requirements by accumulating comparative studies of similar regions.

Summary of this Section

Here, let us summarize the discussion in this section Takano (2016) showed that based on the premise of equal distribution of shops according to the supply principle of the central place theory of Christaller, (1) a cycle of entry and exit and (2) community businesses that accept high toll levels are established in depopulated areas. The purpose of this paper was to examine whether this is true even in the depopulated areas of Hiroshima Pref.

In the narrow sense perspective, the answer to this question was completed in a single word "Not applicable." However, based on the results of Takano (2016), the three principles of Christaller and the three environmental factors surrounding the region are summarized, and the following results (Table 3.1) are obtained from a broad perspective. First, with regard to consumer behavior, Takano's case is a new movement (①) of the supply principle (K = 3) and its form of community business is linked to the community economy. In addition, the Sera case seems to be a bud of community economy by correction (②) of traffic principle (K = 4). The Jinseki-kogen Fureai taxi is what appeared in the administrative principle (K = 7) (③) and, like Sera case, is linked to the community economy (⑤) . And almost all of the surveyed towns in Hiroshima Pref. were strongly influenced by the strategic location of commercial capital (④).

Table 7-1 Comparison of relationships between three principles of Christellar's central place theory and three changes in the environment surrounding the region			
	the transforma- tion of consumer behavior	the strategic location of the commercial capital	the information and communications revolution → another economy
supply principle (= K3 system)	①community business (Takano's model)→⑤ community economy	④All municipalities under Hiroshima pref. are strongly affected (→ uniform arrangement collapse). · Sera : Integration on Route 432 · Jinseki-kogen : Suction to surrounding municipalities (Sanwa→Fukuyama, Jinseki →Tojo,Fuchu,Sera)	⑤ community economy (another economy)
traffic principle (= K4 system)	②Mobile sales & Tsuna shop (Sera)→⑤ community economy		
administrative principle (= K7 system)	③Jinseki Fureai Taxi →⑤ community economy		

Table 3.1. Comparison of Relationship between Three Principles of Christellar's Central Place Theory and Three Changes in the Environment Surrounding the Region

Let's dig a little deeper into the underlying logical structure of this phenomenon and the idea of what supports it. The relationship between each is shown in Figure 3.2. First is the consumer behavior in depopulated areas. The "strategic location of commercial capital" in Figure 3.2 had a large effect on the location of commercial stores (The case in Kagoshima needs to be examined separately, but it is assumed that the same influence is received here). The strategic location by this commercial capital influenced the placement of commercial stores in the depopulated area, but as the solid arrow shows, it acted on each layer of the three principles of the Christaller and gave different results. For this layer-by-layer action, the answer given out in the region was the community business (Takano's model) in the depopulated areas in the supply principle and mobile services (Sera-cho, Jinseki-kogen-cho) in the traffic principle. These two cases are all reactions from the area by the power of the private sector based on reciprocity and it has the character as a vector towards community economy as a new trend of the times (or solidarity, as shown by the dashed arrow because of its reciprocity).

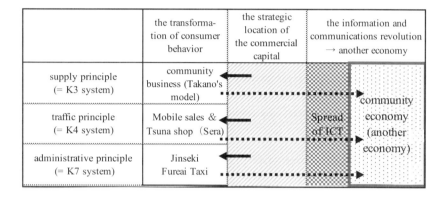

	the transformation of consumer behavior	the strategic location of the commercial capital	the information and communications revolution → another economy
supply principle (= K3 system)	community business (Takano's model)		community economy (another economy)
traffic principle (= K4 system)	Mobile sales & Tsuna shop (Sera)	Spread of ICT	
administrative principle (= K7 system)	Jinseki Fureai Taxi		

Figure 3.2. The Relation between Three Principles of Christellar's Central Place Theory and Three Changes in the Environment Surrounding the Region

Moreover, as the information and communication revolution was explained by Dr. Hagino at the beginning of this study with the example of Amami, the influence is becoming apparent in the depopulated areas of Kagoshima Pref. Amami's example is the sight of the former Amami ferry, where shoppers who went out to Maruya Garden in Kagoshima city and bought lots of products such as UNIQLO and returned home were standard. But now, it is changing to the pile of cardboard of Amazon and Rakuten that the carrier shipped. Due to time constraints, it is impossible to go into this part in detail in this Hiroshima survey. But, it is commonly confirmed that home delivery use is increasing mainly for the young generation in the interview in the field. Similar to passenger cars, mobile devices and the Internet are essential items in depopulated areas, and as in Kagoshima Pref., in Hiroshima Pref., the information and communication infrastructure has become the common infrastructure of a new era essential for life.

On the other hand, Jinseki-Kogen-cho was under the influence of a nearby commercial area, and its commercial area was divided, making it difficult to secure public transport in the area. Through repeated trials and errors, Jinseki-Kogen-cho has created a transportation service called "Jinseki Fureai Taxi" that assumes unrestricted free operation. Due to the difficulty of public transportation in a wide area, this service has the property of a valuable public infrastructure as well as information and communication infrastructure for residents.

Because it is equally given to those who meet the requirements, if this service is considered as a common activity base used by one-sixth of the whole town people's population, it will be possible to create a lot of added value to this mechanism. For example, various services such as simple sales of daily necessities in taxis, various agency services by taxi drivers and marketing such as questionnaire surveys at the time of use can be considered.

In addition, since daily usage databases can analyse usage behavior such as hospitals, shopping, and meals, it is possible to bundle services such as switching to a home visit method every meeting place on a weekly basis based on the analysis results. Plus, as an application of this system, it will be possible to invite residents to an exchange project by grasping the behavior dynamics such as learning things, a circle of hobbies, and interaction with different generations. The freedom of movement enhances the activities of the residents. If this is used as a communication infrastructure, it will also open the way for the super-elderly to participate in society. Such an approach could also serve as a model to show that depopulated areas with many issues are advanced areas for solving problems.

Finally, let us summarize the development of the remaining inverse Lewis Theory to another economy (⑤) in the next section.

On the Sprouting of a New Economic Cycle from Inverse Lewis Theory to Another Economy

On the rapid progress of science, technology, and capitalism, Arendt said, "the apparatuses we once handled freely begin to look as though they were shells belonging to the human body as the shell belongs to the body of a turtle" (Arendt, 1958, p.153). She also rang a warning bell the development of technology encourages the proliferation of 'labor', and swallows 'work', and has an inherent risk of inhibiting human 'activity'. Meanwhile, philosopher Marx Gabriel explains the characteristics of modern capitalism as follows. Marxism describes the development of history in the class struggle, and psychoanalysis describes the mental illness caused by that class struggle, so combining them may explain all social phenomena. Furthermore, as psychologist Jacques Lacan says, an infant (human) confronted with his helplessness reflected in a mirror recovers the destroyed self-image by projecting the image of another person. And if you make this constant projection mechanism your own, that is, if you can control the construction of self-image in the community, you can control or control class struggle. Thus, neoliberalism has fully accepted the theoretical teachings of early Marxism and psychoanalysis, turning it into a huge advertising industry. Because the advertising industry is an industry that projects images and self-images. Similarly, Gabriel sees that the cultural industry also controls the building of self-image in the community and controls or controls class struggle. (Matsuyama, 2018a, pp.126-135). It is the "cultural industry" described by Theodor Adorno and Max Horkheimer in The Dialectics of Enlightenment (Horkheimer and Adorno, 1947). Thus, these critics warn that the rapid development of technology in capitalism will unite the device itself with the human body as a part of the turtle shell and also industrialize the human-made culture.

On the other hand, according to the French economist Daniel Cohen, in the transition from agriculture to industry in the development process of capitalism, the industry became the recipient of agriculture and absorbed its surplus population. It is the result of compensating for the gap between the two by simultaneously occurring technological innovation and industrial technological innovation (Maruyama, 2018b, p.34). On top of that, "IT and AI etc., are rapidly developing and since the industry that is the saucer advances technological innovation without revealing a clear form, unlike the transition from agriculture to industry, there are many intermediate. It is pointed out that "the wealth is concentrated to the few who dominate the technology while the layer is taken away," (p.36). Thus, capitalism and in particular the logic of neoliberalism creates an economy in which desires produce desires (Maruyama, 2018a, p.63), changing the culture to part of the industry and dismantling the middle class, brings the polarization phenomenon to society.

For the former movement (in Arendt's language, "labor unity"), Arendt describes how art resists, and "helper of the highest ability < operator", i.e, artist, poet, history editor. They need the help of monument builders and writers, because without their help the products of their activity, the stories they play and tell, will never survive" (Arendt, 1958). Paradoxically, it suggests that art is a sort of bridgehead. On the other hand, drawing Freud's words that "artists are always exposed to a lack of creativity ('frustration in culture')," Cohen pointed out the difficulty of saying that modern people are under heavy pressure to replace computers with only non-routine work, that is, to constantly innovate like artists (Maruyama, 2018b, p.52).

Regarding the latter post-capitalist, another economy, public interest capitalism is discussed in business science. Looking at the major flow of capitalism from the viewpoint of business administration, it is transitioning from commercial capitalism to industrial capitalism and to post-capitalism.

In industrial capitalism, profit comes from mass production and low wages, but in post-capitalism, corporate innovation generates profit. As supply is enough, earning becomes the point. With innovation, we will give out what is sought in the world. Innovation, if well done, produces significant benefits while promoting the dichotomy of income. In a capitalist society, money produces money and promotes the gap between rich and not rich. For the public interest, capitalism is debated from the question of whether this is good or not. The argument is that it is better to bring to a wider return so that the return will not be concentrated on a specific shareholder.

Connected to that, it is also a governance theory. A specific example is a kind of employee-owned company such as Metro in Germany, Tesco in the UK, John Lewis, Marks & Spencer. Besides this, Mondragon in Spain and Peoples Market in the United Kingdom take the form of labor investment. Work several months a month at the same time as a worker contributes.

Towards post-capitalism and another economy, there is a remarkable solidarity economy debate in France, and a movement of community economy based on communities and nature, while ensuring equal opportunities and reallocation of stock. First, let's look at the movement of the solidarity economy. Kawaguchi (2013) examines the city of Roubaix in the Lille metropolitan area in France. First, it considers the development of measures to expand employment and social participation centered on a social solidarity economy. It was clarified that the city had been rehabilitated by the urban regeneration strategy by changing to industry. Here, there is the recognition that the market economy is embedded in society, the economy spans the non-market economy (redistribution) and reciprocity, and the solidarity economy is an "economy based on reciprocity". In addition, Tatemi (2018) also analysed the formation process of the solidarity economy in France in detail and deducted Dacheux et Goujion (2015), the positioning of the current solidarity economy, firstly, the liberal trojan hoarse as part of the capitalist rule that we see as the second place. Next, views the solidarity economy as a transition to "ethical" capitalism or cognitive capitalism, and lastly, into post-capitalism. It is classified into three transitions and perspectives. As for the future of the solidarity economy, while taking into consideration the possibility of the "other economy" (second and third positions), the first concern is not clear, so the local practice is multi-layered (microdevices) and institutional environment maintenance (macro devices) in a larger framework has implications.

Moreover, standing watch the movement of rural return in Japan from the analogy of the approach of the solidarity economy in France. While Japan's declining birthrate and aging population bring about the warning of disappearing cities (Masuda's report), the 3.11 shock lead to more young people aiming at the local area, and in relation to local social relations and resources, the migrants have their own Nariwai in Japanese. This is because there is a movement to build new relationships and networks in a way that supports it. This is one of the phenomena that can be regarded as a related population or an active population. Tatemi also predicts a bridge between solidarity economics and rural regressions, mediated by the Neo-endogenous development of Odagiri, also utilizing actor-network theory(ANT) and convention theory (Tatemi and Tsutsui, 2018).

The community economy is another form of post-capitalism. Hiroi (2015) focuses on the direction of socialization that goes back to the roots of capitalism. It focuses on the missing "communities" and "locals" while providing the perspective of "equal opportunities" and "redistribution of stock" through social security in the first half of life. He argues that one possible vision is not to take off the market economy indefinitely, but rather to reconnect it to the underlying foundation of "community" and "nature" before landing. He insists that such an economic society should be oriented and realized. From this perspective, Hiroi suggests the possibility of a community economy. Hiroi (2015) relies on Polanyi (1944) and classifies public, mutual, and private into three: public = reciprocity (community), public = redistribution (government), and private = exchange (market). In addition, the region/nation/earth will be explained from region = local, nation = national, and earth = global. This restores reciprocity (community) in a modern way and corrects the redistribution of "public" and the distortion of "I" and exchange. Hiroi's idea is similar to the consideration in this paper, which recovers the distortions applied to each layer of the supply principle, traffic principle, and administrative principle by the action of the strategic location of commercial agglomeration by the reciprocity-based reaction. It is similar to the community business analyzed by Takano (2016) and is compatible with new movements in Hiroshima Prefecture.

On the other hand, the solidarity economy, which originated from charitable solidarity derived from the charity of the church, expanded to all activities in the 1990s after the discussion of "another economy" in the 1960s, and to social activities in 2014, The Solidarity Economic Relations Act is now being enacted (Standing 2018). As described above, the solidarity economy has its own history and institutional structure. There is no guarantee that transplanting the system to Japan will work. The solidarity economy also has concerns about neoliberal Trojan horses as pointed out by Dacheux et Goujion (2015). In light of this situation, while referring to the discussion, of the solidarity economy, we will first connect Takano (2016) and the results of this Hiroshima survey to the discussion of Hiroi's community economy and repeat case analysis in each region. It would be appropriate to elaborate, the theory frame in the course of this research. This matches the problem awareness of this paper, asking the conditions for establishing community businesses in depopulated areas.

In this survey, for example, Osaki-Kamijima-cho, where migrants gather, such as a couple of I-turn who runs a fisherman's cafe, a young man who has been trained by a plasterer from France, a young woman who opened a glass workshop, etc. There are various things such as a pizzeria, a fish shop and a marché. New stores and owners, such as the navel cafe in Sera Town, are also bringing renewal to Sera Town. Including the pan shop "Navel Cafe" by this immigrant from Spain, there are currently about 10 old-fashioned cafes in nearly 10 houses in Sera Town. These are, in particular, scattered around the edge of Sera Town. There are similarities and affinity with the leaders of the sixth industry such as Okada Farm. Their sales form is close to that of Takano (2016). These also give important hints to the formation of "regional image" in the countryside.

In Peace Winds Japan (PWJ)'s activities in Jinseki Kogencho, including Peace Wanko Japan Project, there will always be around 120 young staff members from outside the town. PWJ is connected with 27 countries in the world through humanitarian assistance activities as an international cooperation NGO and we can expect to interact with many people from inside and outside the country that visit Jinseki-kogen-cho. Such movements are also linked to the community economy in the context of rural return. Thus, the broad perspective obtained in the process of this case study is to lead the study results of community business in Takano (2016) and the result of this Hiroshima survey to the study of the community economy. Besides, advancing research from such a viewpoint also leads to growing and developing the inverse Lewis theory into a more fruitful one.

Finally, let's check the remaining issues. In this Hiroshima survey, it was confirmed that the uniform distribution of stores based on the principle of supply of Christaller was distorted at strategic locations of commercial capital and many collapsed. However, the process of transformation was not demonstrated. For example, if you plot the small country and Tsuna shops in the former Sera Nishi-cho, organize the time and reason for closing the shop, and summarize the background situation with ethnic methods in interviews with neighbors, etc. The relationship with the store consolidation becomes clearer. In the past, it would be possible to find out when and why they were lost from the same town where bars and snacks were crowded. Furthermore, in this study, it was impossible to clarify the reason why the former Toyomatsu-son, which was confirmed to maintain the uniform layout based on the Christaller's supply principle, was maintained. Including such a detailed analysis of the issues, I would like to continue to follow the path of this research.

References:

Aoyama yuko, Murphey T. James, Hanson susan,2011, *Key Concepts in Economic Geography*.London:Sage

Arendt Hannah, 1958, *The Human Condition*, Chicago& London : The University of Chicago Press.

Christaller Walter, 1933, *Die zentrlen Orte in Suddentschaft*, Jena : G.Fischer.

Hiroi Yoshinori, 2015, *Posuto sihonsyugi* (Post capitalism), Tokyo : Iwanami Shoten.

Horkheimer Max, Adorno Theodor, 1947, *Dialektik der Auflärung : Philosophishe Fragmente*, Amsterdam: Querido Verlag.

Kawaguchi Natuki, 2013, Development of a social and solidarity economy and urban regeneration in Roubaix, France, *Japanese Journal of Human Geography* Vol.65 No.4, pp.40-56.

Maruyama Shunichi, 2018a, *Yokubo no zidaiwo tetugakusuru* (Philosophy in the age of desire), Tokyo:NHK shupan.

Maruyama Shunichi, 2018b, *Shihonsyugi 2* (Capitalism 2), Tokyo: Toyokeizai shimposha .

Matsubara Hiroshi , 2013, chushinchi riron no kiso to oyou （Fundamentals and applications of central place theory） , *Gendai no ritchiron* （*Modern location theory*） , Tokyo : kokinsyoin, pp.38-53.

Nishimura Satoru and Hagino Makoto, 2019, Fiflh Regional Development International Workshop— Searching forRegional Characteristics of Community Businesses—

Polanyi, Karl, 1944, *The Great Transfomation : The Political and Economic Origins of Our Time,* UK : Victor Gollancz.

Takano, Tetuya, 2016, A study on some condition to subsist community business in depopulated area : An Approach analysis of islands area and the inland area Satsumasendai City（doctoral dissertation）, Kagoshima University.

Tatemi Junya, 2018, Development of social and solidarity economy in France : un Experiment toward "un Alternative Economy"*Management Research* （Bulletin of Osaka City University) Vol.69 No.2, pp.19-39.

Tatemi Junya and Tsutsui Shinichi, 2018, Denenkaiki to rentaikeizai no setten wo saguru(Exploring the connection between rural return and solidarity economy) *Japanese Journal of Geography 2018 Jun*,) pp.63-66.

BAZAAR AND COMMUNITY BUSINESS

SUEO KUWAHARA

Center for General Education
Kagoshima University

Introduction

According to Encyclopedia Britannica, Bazaar is originally a public marketplace or street of a Persian town, where goods and services are exchanged or sold. The term originates from the Persian word *bāzār*. From Persia, the term spread to Arabia, where the Arabic word *sūq* is synonymous as it meant "the place where the price is determined". Commonly, there is no "set price" in bazaar, that is, "multiple prices for one product" in which the buyer and the seller negotiate per product or per trade and different prices are decided per buyer.

In North America and some European countries, the term can be used as a synonym for a "rummage sale", to describe charity fundraising events held by churches or other community organizations in which either donated used goods such as books, clothes, and household items, or new and handcrafted goods are sold for low prices. It is applied both to a single shop or concession selling miscellaneous articles and to a fair at which such miscellany is sold, sometimes for charity (Haneda 1999: 16-18).

In this article, after the function of bazaar was reviewed from the previous studies, the cases of bazaars in the Philippines and Tanzania will be discussed from the viewpoint of community business.

Historical Background of Bazaar

In ancient Mesopotamia and West Asia, necessities including food were stored and distributed at the gate of the palace and walled city, and handicrafts were sold in bazaar. For a long time, the gate and bazaar played an institutional role in distributing necessities of everyday life. After the commerce of the Islamic world became widespread, the function of the local food market was added to the bazaar of a handicraftsman. Finally, the bazaar undertook the sales function of foreign goods (Polanyi 1980: 247).

The basic structure of bazaar is that permanent stores line up on both sides of the street. When it developed, crossroads were made and stores increased along the streets which are crossed and paralleled. Permanent stores served both sales and craftsman's workshops. By gathering the same profession in each section, bazaar had advantages such as fair trade through competition and making administration easier (Sakamoto 1999).

Away from the permanent stores, there were facilities called "*salai*" or "*caravan salai*" which were used for lodging, warehouse or remote trade. In the doorway of the street, there was a square, around which there were *mosque*, *madrasa*, and *hammam* (public bathhouse). The square was used for various purposes such as religious festivals, periodic market and so on. As the rental charge for the trade in the square was unnecessary, even the street vendors, peddlers and farmers who couldn't have the permanent stores could take part in the square. Perishable food such as vegetables and fruits and domestic animals were traded in the square. Furthermore, flea market for selling unnecessary things was held (Sakamoto 1999).

Many present-day bazaars are the places where shops were piled up to trade spices, fabrics, salt, gold and so on. Normally, the wholesales and retailers of the same competing business are piled up on the roofed street around the mosque in the town (Haneda 1999: 16-18).

In the bazaar, there was a meeting of suppliers and consumers, but that was not for the food market, but for the craftsman's crafts. Sales were not done outside but in the roofed shops. Unlike the modern markets, every item in bazaar had multiple prices, the organization was solid, and the competition was eliminated. The important point is that in the modern price formation market, the price was determined by supply and demand, and there was a single price for one thing whereas bazaar lacked a clear market element (single price) from the beginning (Polanyi 1980: 246-247).

Bazaar as a Complex Space

In the traditional bazaar of Iran, the entrance is not clear and hard to find. However, the flow of people would often bring you to the bazaar without knowing. Inside the bazaar, there is a dark and dim passage in which brick domed vaults continue. Other than brick, there is the case of a roof covered with tin or wood, which is designed to avoid the winter wind and rain. In both sides of the passage, small shops with a narrow frontage and depth are lined up tightly. The shop owners' houses are located in other districts. Presently, each shop has a shutter, but in the past, the large door at the entrance was closed in the evening when business was over (Haneda1999: 16-18).

Almost all kinds of products for everyday life are sold in bazaar. However, perishable food such as meat and vegetables are often sold at the different sections and an open-air market in the square. The bazaar in Iran is mostly a wholesaler street. Miscellaneous goods and handicrafts are main items, but expensive goods such as precious metals and jewelry are sold at times. Commercial goods such as hardware, leather shoes, bag, and fabrics are assigned to every different section. Since many of the shops that deal with the same goods are gathered into one section, customers can buy cheaper and better goods while comparing the goods of different shops (Kamioka & Yoshieda 1999: 65-66; Haneda 1999: 17-18). In the bazaars in Iran, shopkeepers try to show off how much they can showcase the products in a small shop. The proof of a good store depends on the number of products such as shoes, dishes, clothing and so on which are showcased in a narrow space from floor to ceiling (Haneda 1999: 17-18).

A bazaar is a pathway with small retail shops and is a more complex commercial space. There is a narrow pathway between shops through which rays of light are shining. Further ahead, a bright spacious space called "Caravan Sarai" appears, which is a courtyard of the facility (Haneda 1999: 18). Other than Caravan Sarai in the bazaar, there are also small entrance gates to religious facilities such as mosque, Madrasa (school dormitory), Imamzada (Saint's mausoleum) and so on, which are facing the pathway (Haneda 1999:18-19).

The bazaar in which commercial and religious facilities exist in the mixture is a complex building consisted of the combination of many buildings. Commercial facilities represented by the bazaar and religious facilities led by a mosque coexist in the center of Iranian towns. Since both of them are public facilities, their location in the center of town was convenient for the residents. However, what connects the two facilities is the donation system called "*Wakufu*" which is unique to the Islamic world (Haneda 1999: 20-22).

The construction of a religious facility was one of the ways for wealthy people to spend their wealth most effectively. Once the religious facility was built, the funds for the operation is required, that is, normally, for carpet renewal, oil for lighting, wax, employee salary, meals for the professors and students of *Madrasa*, building repair and maintenance and so on. Those who build religious facilities had to prepare these funds and allowance beforehand. In that case, the most frequently used way was to build commercial facilities such as bazaar and Caravan *Sarai* together with the religious facility (Haneda 1999: 23).

The bazaar stores and the rooms of Caravan Sarai were rented out, and the revenue that the necessary expenses were subtracted from the rent was allocated for the cost of management and operation of the *mosque*. Religious and commercial facilities were built in bulk by the same constructor. The existence of the religious and commercial facilities was assured by being built together (Haneda 1999: 23).

Iran has prospered by taking the hegemony of the east-west relay trade since ancient times. In the state, the *Ekiden* system and facilities such as Caravan *Sarai* which was the accommodation of caravan were developed. In such a situation, the bazaar was not just a place for buying and selling goods but has been playing the role as a place for major information exchange among the merchants whose origin and language were different (Yoshieda 1999: 88).

The more the kind of distributing product and the width of information expand, the more the bazaar prospers. The bazaar in the town near the border is full of liveliness. Except Persian, the languages here are those of people who crossed the border and the dialects of the place (Yoshieda 1999: 89). A bazaar is a place not just to do the shopping but to enjoy meeting people (Kamioka & Yoshieda 1999: 70).

In the cases of Marrakech, the bazaars of Morocco with old history, shoppers go through the tiled gate and enter the bazaar, which is the narrow path maze overflowing with shoppers, and the senses of shoppers are overwhelmed by the strong scent of spices and the stunning colors of goods, the screams of mule riders. Craftsmen are forming groups according to products such as ceramics, shoes, brass products, wooden products, sculptures, clothing, basket, marquetry and so on (Macmillan 2007: 57).

Merchants and Customers

Anthropologist Clifford Geertz says that the information in bazaar is highly credible, though the way of its transmission is poor, rare, ubiquitous and inefficient. There are full of things that we don't understand such as the quality of the product, current price level, the possibility of market establishment, product cost and so on. Price including the cheapest one is not shown, nor the trademark and advertisement. The experienced buyers search the information widely and try to protect themselves not to be claimed an unreasonably high price nor to be charged for low-quality products. Shoppers spend time comparing the products offered by the various merchants, whereas the merchants spend time in persuading customers to buy at their shops. According to Geertz, the search for information is the core experience in their lives in bazaar, and the only truly advanced technology in bazaar and everything depends on it (Geertz 1978:29-31).

Since many of the merchants of brass products are accumulated in one area in Marrakech, it takes less than a few seconds to walk from one merchant to the other. So, customers often compare the prices while walking one to the other. Travelers are no match for merchants in bazaar, and they often buy at a higher price than necessary. The merchants of bazaar are tough negotiators with experiences, whereas most travelers lack the general knowledge about the standard price level and the ability to judge the quality of the crafts, thus, they often pay an extortionate price (Macmillan 2007: 58-59).

The local people who shop regularly at the bazaar are in different situations from travelers. Though the local people are also facing the transaction cost and lacking the knowledge about the products and prices, there is a countervailing power for the merchants to discourage high pricing against the local people. That is, the merchants are thinking to continue their business there (Macmillan 2007: 62).

Different from travelers, the regular bazaar customers construct a relationship with specific merchants. They roughly negotiate with various merchants and check the current price, but finally, they always go back to the serious deal with usual merchants. This is the connection by convenience, but sellers and buyers are still hostile. Shoppers seek a low price and merchants seek a high price. Sellers and buyers negotiate hard overtime. However, their interests are not completely conflicting. Shoppers highly regard that the relationship with the merchant provides security that is not deceived, and merchants think that they want to satisfy customers to the extent that they visit their shops tomorrow again. The relationship between the both, save exploration costs and result in lower prices for the repeaters (Macmillan 2007: 63).

Bazaar and Community Business

The small general stores in the Philippines known as *sari-sari stores* are said to be an important source of income for people in poverty, and that many shop owners make a significant contribution to the micro-economy at a grass-roots level. In the Philippines, a type of bazaar known as *tiangge* is more important for the low-income earners in cities than small general stores such as *sari-sari stores*, and the business entities such as *sari-sari* stores which support the urban and rural life supplementary can be taken as community business (Nishimura & Hagino, 2019).

In Tanzania, small stores called *duka* to play a supplementary role to bazaars. Community businesses there are characterized in the form of shops which sell virtually everything in retails, weekly organizer open bazaar called "Gulio" and other forms. The *Gulio* represents a weekly organized open market in Tanzania. Anyone can participate in the market, which is characterized by the absence of tariffs, taxes, licensing requirements, subsidies, unionization, and any other regulations or practices that interfere with naturally functioning operations (Busungu and Kessy 2019).

In rural Tanzania, *Gulio* is one of the major economic activities. The space or location of the *Gulio* is composed of temporary structures and it is determined by the local government. The rural communities, traders and middlemen bring their goods and services at the *Gulio*. The products of the rural communities are mostly rice, vegetables, maize, chicken, yogurt and tobacco. The traders are mostly small scale petty traders and bring industrial goods like cloth, domestic utensils, electronics while middlemen bring either agricultural products or industrial products. In an open market, the pricing of goods or services depends predominantly on the principles of supply and demand with limited interference or outside influence from governmental agencies. A well functioning *Gulio* in Tanzania is the health indicator of economic prosperity, strong community business and rural resilience (Busungu and Kessy 2019).

In rural Tanzania, *Gulio* is one of the major economic activities. Although it is weekly organized, it represents a high opportunity for rural community businesses to sell, showcases their products and services, higher interaction with customers, and establishment of business networks. From *Gulio*, the community gets more satisfaction and buys more volumes of goods and services per day. Rural people get utmost satisfaction through the weekly organized bazaar "Gulio". The importance of weekly organized bazaar "Gulio" in rural areas is in several factors which include the availability of a wide range of products and services, cheapest price, a high chance of offers and natural environment which permits high interaction and leisure for the rural people (Busungu and Kessy 2019).

To understand community business that supports people's daily life, a good understanding of the function of bazaar would be also needed. As Geertz pointed above, shoppers spend a lot of time in bazaar to collect various information to protect themselves from being charged to an unreasonably high price or being cheated to buy low-quality products, whereas merchants spend time to attract the customers and persuade them to buy the products.

Future Tasks

In the bazaar of Iran and the Islamic world, unlike the modern market, there are multiple prices in every product, and competition is excluded. In the modern price formation market, the price depends on supply and demand, and there is a single price for one product. The bazaar lacks a clear market element (single price) from the beginning. The information search for finding prices is the core experience as the essence of a bazaar.

In the strict sense that we saw above, we could say that bazaar does not exist in Japan, the Philippine and Tanzania. However, Tanzania's market called *Gulio* in which agricultural and industrial products are simply laid along the street seems to be closer to the features of the original bazaar. Re-examining bazaars in the Philippines and Tanzania from the viewpoint of information search, which is the core experience in bazaar, would be desirable.

References:

Busungu, Constantine and Delphine Kessy, 2019, Serving rural communities: Deciphering the roles of community businesses in providing basic goods and services to rural communities

Geertz, Clifford, 1978 "The Bazaar Economy: Information and Search in Peasant Marketing", *The American Economic Review* 68(2): 28-32.

Haneda, Masashi, 1999, Toshi no souchi (Urban equipment),Kamioka, K. ed., *Kurashi ga wakaru ajia dokuhon* (in Japanese), Tokyo: Kawadeshobo, pp. 16 -23.

Kamioka Koji and Satoko Yoshieda 1999, Teheran no bazaar (Bazaar in Teheran), *Kurashi ga wakaru ajia dokuhon* (in Japanese), Tokyo: Kawadeshobo, pp. 68 -70.

Macmillan, John, 2006, *Shijo wo tsukuru: Bazaar kara netto torihiki made* (in Japanese), Tokyo: Iwanami Shoten

Nishimura, Satoru and Makoto Hagino, 2019, Fifth Regional Development International Workshop— Searching for Regional Characteristics of Community Businesses—

Polanyi, Karl, 1980(1977), *Ningen no Keizai I&II* (in Japanese), Tokyo:Iwanami Shoten

Sakamoto, Tsutomu, 1999, Isuramu toshi no shijo kukan to Isfahan (Market space of Islamic cities and Isfahan), Sato, K. and Kishimoto, M.eds., *Shijo no chiiki-shi* (in Japanese), Tokyo: Yamakawa Shuppan

Yoshimura, Satoko, Perusha-go ga wakarimasen (I don't know Persian), Kamioka, K. ed., *Kurashi ga wakaru ajia dokuhon* (in Japanese), Tokyo: Kawadeshobo, pp. 82-89.

Kojie, 6th edition, 2008

Daijisen, 2nd edtion, 2012

ENCYCLOPEDIA BRITANNICA: https://www.britannica.com

THE PROLIFERATION AND DOMINATION OF COMMUNITY BUSINESS IN THE PHILIPPINES: THE CASE OF FILIPINO SARI-SARI STORES IN A RURAL NEIGHBORHOOD

ROMEO PEÑA[1] AND TOMOAKI TAKESHITA[2]

[1]Polytechnic University of the Philippines
[2]Kagoshima University

Introduction

In the Philippines, no single socioeconomic institution in the country today boasts a greater numerical presence in the Philippine community than a sari-sari store. Sari-sari stores dot the neighborhood landscape so profusely that sometimes only a single house separates from another (Silverio 1982). The observation is just as true today because the Philippine FMCG (fast-moving consumer goods) market is still dominated by "sari-sari" stores. It accounts for almost seventy percent (70%) sales of manufactured consumer goods, which makes it a valuable part of the economy and an important conduit for making vital goods available to Filipino neighborhood communities. According to the study of Bonnin (2006), he observed that it was not unusual in the Philippines to find four or five stores within the same block, and in one instance, three stores were located side-by-side in adjacent homes.

We are addressing the question—why do sari-sari stores still dominate in the FMCG market although retailers have been modernized?—in terms of the relationship between micro-business and communities. In this research, we chose Barangay Tagabas Ibaba in Quezon Province as the research field according to the following three reasons:

1. Unlike Metro Manila, we can specify boundaries between small communities in terms of geographic features.

2. This Barangay is characterized by coconut farming. The coconut industry is one of the main agricultural industries in the Philippines and coconuts characterize Filipino culture and society, so we can think the area is one of the typical rural areas.

3. Despite it, other researchers have not researched this area, so this research should have a value of description.

It is about 260 kilometers from Manila City to Tagabas Ibaba, taking 6 hours and more by car to get there. Tagabas Ibaba is located in Bondoc Peninsula in the southeast of Quezon Province (Figure 5.1). In the western part of the Barangay, a road with two branches of about three kilometers leads from the South to the North. The only inhabitable areas are along the road and they account merely for nine percent in the whole area of the Barangay. In this small Barangay, which consists of four *Sitios* (Doongan Silangan, Central Silangan, Doongan Kanluran, and Central Kanluran), less than 2,000 people live ten kilometers from the nearest town, the center of the municipality of Catanauan (Table 5.1, Figure 5.2).

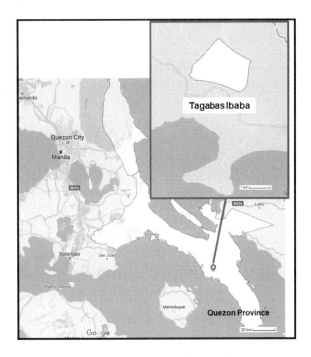

Figure 5.1. Barangay Tagabas Ibaba
Note. Made by the authors from Google Map, retrieved from https://www.google.com

item	size
Population (2015)	1,837
Whole area	430 ha
Inhabitable area	37.5 ha
Length of the road	2.9 km

Table 5.1. Basic information on Tagabas Ibaba
Note. Data for Population from PSA, retrieved from
http://www.psa.gov.ph/ and for areas from author's measure

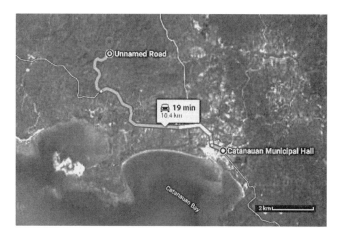

Figure 5.2. Distance from Tagabas Ibaba to the Nearest Town
Note. Made by the authors from Google Map,
Retrieved from https://www.google.com

The authors conducted two kinds of research: (1) gathering coordinates of each sari-sari store in the Barangay and (2) questionnaires for all the sari-sari stores and for some customers living there. In this section, we will see the status quo and findings on sari-sari store in Tagabas Ibaba.

Profiles of the Sari-Sari Stores in Tagabas Ibaba

The complete survey into all the sari-sari stores in the Barangay revealed profiles of the stores or the store owners. From the view of marital status and sex, we can say that sari-sari stores there are typical housewife-business. Nineteen (19) stores out of the 21 are managed by wives (married women), 1 store, by a couple, and the rest, by a husband (Table 5.2). Let's look at some cases. An owner started her store after she got married and quitted her previous Job, a clerk of a drug store. Another used to be a teacher at the high school in the same Barangay but she had to quit the job because she had to take care of her mother who had heart disease, and then chose to establish a sari-sari store; for she was able to manage it while looking after her mother. Over half (59.1%) of them belong to the middle-aged range (40-49 and 50-59; figure 5.3).

	frequency	percentage
wife	19	90.5%
husband	1	4.8%
couple	1	4.8%
sum	21	100.0%

Note: Data from our research.

Table 5.2. The Person Manages the Store

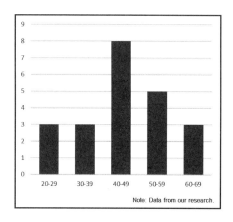

Note: Data from our research.

Figure 5.3. Age Frequency of the Store Owners

In terms of academic background, one-third of owners have a college-level academic background, and the second frequent answers were "high school" (table 5.3). They have a better academic background than we expected, but we couldn't find that their average sales or operation years are much the same as the average of all the stores in this Barangay.

	frequency	persentage
college/univ.	7	33.3%
high school	6	28.6%
elementary	4	19.0%
no answer	4	19.0%
sum	21	100.0%

Note. Data from our research.

Table 5.3. Academic Background of the Owners

How long have the 21 stores operated their stores? The answers to this question range from less than 8 months to as many as 40 years and their average is 10.2 years (table 5.4). The stores with their operation years within 5 years account for 42.8 percent. This fact implies that it is easy to enter the *sari-sari* store market there.

operation years	frequency
1-5	9
(1-2)	(7)
6-10	7
11-15	1
16-20	0
21-25	1
26-30	2
31-35	0
36-40	1
average	10.2 years

Note. Data from our research.

Table 5.4. Length of Operation

About licenses, surprisingly 20 stores out of 21 (95.2 percent) secure them from the municipality. The rest of them have permission from the Barangay Chairman. In this Barangay, almost all of the sari-sari stores are legally operated, so they belong to the formal sector.

Market Area Analysis of Sari-Sari Stores

As mentioned, 21 sari-sari stores are found in Tagabas Ibaba (Figure 5.4). Aside from sari-sari stores, there are as few as two B-to-C establishments (a toy stall and a canteen; Table 5.5). This shows us that only a sari-sari store can *virtually* subsist as a B-to-C business there. The fact that there are 21 sari-sari stores in the area where only 1,837 people live implies that the *sari-sari* store's threshold—minimum demand—is very small. Concretely speaking, we can think that the yardstick of the threshold is population per sari-sari store from which the owner's family is subtracted: 82.9 people (Table 5.6). Also, the number of households per sari-sari store is 19, which means a sari-sari store can be supported by the demand of 18 households, and one household runs a sari-sari store every 19 households. If the profitability of the sari-sari stores is at breakeven point—the point in which costs equal sales—, the number of 82.9 people means exactly the demand threshold, but when we asked the store owners how to use profit, most of them answered that they could re-invest, for example, they can use their profit for increasing inventory (100%), saving (81%) and buying store equipment (57.1%; Table 5.7). This result implies that most of the stores are profitable or above the breakeven point. Therefore, the true demand threshold may be still smaller than 82.9 people.

Figure 5.4. Examples of Sari-Sari Stores in Tagabas Ibaba

Note. Pictures taken by the authors.

91

B to C establishment	23
sari-sari store	21
typical	20
with canteen	1
canteen	1
toy stall	1

Public establishment	3
school	2
elementary school	1
high school	1
barangay hall	1

Note. These data from our research.

Table 5.5. Number of Sari-Sari Stores and the other Establishments

	item	size
A	Population	1,837
B	The number of housholds (estimated)	399
C	Sari-sari store	21
D	The average household size (Canatauan)	4.6
A/C	Poppulation per sari-sari store	87.5
A/C–D	Yardstic of demand threshold (people)	82.9
B/C	Households per sari-sari store	19
B/C–1	Yardstick of demand threshold (households)	18

Note. B estimated by the average household size in Catanauan (4.6) from PSA, retrieved from http://www.psa.gov.ph/

Table 5.6. Indices of the Sari-Sari Store Market in Tagabas Ibaba

where to use profit	frequency	percentage
daily life	21	100.0%
saving	17	81.0%
store equipment	12	57.1%
increasing inventory	21	100.0%
education fee	18	85.7%
other business	1	4.8%

Note. Data from our research.

Table 5.7. Profit Usage

Then, let's take a look at market areas of sari-sari stores especially. Figure 5.5 is the map of sari-sari stores made by gathered GPS data, which shows that sari-sari stores line with the road. Only on the road of 2.9 kilometers, there are 21 of sari-sari stores, so the average distance between sari-sari stores there can be computed at 138.1 meters. To see how dense the sari-sari stores there are, let's compare this with convenience stores in 23 wards of Tokyo or the center of Tokyo, where convenience stores are located most densely in Japan. According to Takemoto (2016), the average distance between convenience stores in the center of Tokyo is 149 meters. This figure is 10.9 meters longer than in the sari-sari store in Tagabas Ibaba, though much the same. Both of them are an about-2-minute walking distance from a sari-sari/convenience store to the next store. So how long are market ranges of them? In order to simplify it, let's suppose that these stores are distributed equally. In Tagabas Ibaba, where sari-sari stores are lined, a market area is divided at the midpoint between two stores, so their average market range should be 69 (138.1/2) meters (Figure 5.6 a). On the other hand, in the center of Tokyo, where convenience stores are specially located, the maximum market radius should be the tangent point to three market areas. It should be 86 (149/ $\sqrt{3}$) meters (Figure 5.6 b). We can say the sari-sari store in Tagabas Ibaba is denser than a convenience store in the center of Tokyo. In any way, since people walk at 60 -80 m/s (Takemoto 2016), people there can go to the nearest sari-sari/convenience store approximately one mi-nute on average.

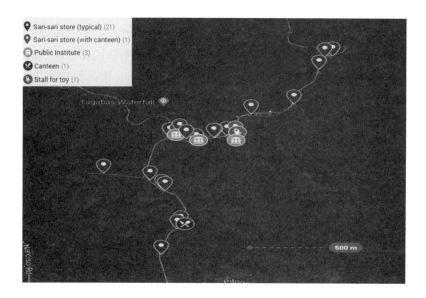

Figure 5.5. Distribution of Sari-sari Stores and the other Establishments

Note. Data from the authors, made from Google my map,
retrieved from https://www.google.com/mymaps

a. Tagabas Ibaba **b. 23 wards of Tokyo**

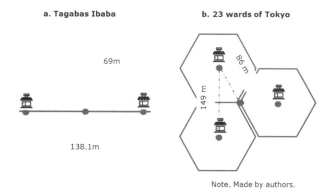

Note. Made by authors.

Figure 5.6. Average Distances of Sari-sari Stores/Convenience Stores

We have discussed market areas of sari-sari stores according to traditional location theories, in which enterprises are monopolistic within their market range, but the actual conditions are not that simple. We asked nine customers how many sari-sari stores they patronize. The average number turned out to be 1.6 stores, and four customers out of nine (44.4%) regularly go to more than one sari-sari stores (Table 5.8).

how many	frequency
1	5
2	3
3	1
average	1.6

Note. Data from the authors

Table 5.8. No. of Sari-Sari Stores Customers Patronize

In the analysis above, the average of whole areas is employed for comparison. We, however, observed that a lot of sari-sari stores accumulated in a specific area in this barangay, or "a cluster." A cluster, which we tentatively named, is a small neighborhood group that consists of about tens of houses (Figure 5.7). A cluster can be specified both by geographical features and by awareness of the residents. Each cluster is separated by unmanned parts of the road, some of which have a slope or a cut-through (Figure 5.8). Each cluster is about 500 meters long (Table 5.9). The nine customers answered that the sari-sari stores that they patronized were in the same cluster. We also asked residents (both store owners and consumers) how many stores opened, closed and used to be there in the neighborhood or the cluster. Their answers were not contradictory to each other, and the answers agreed with our zoning by the geographical features. In addition, we asked all of the owners where their customers come from, and all of them (100%) answered that almost all of their customers came from the same cluster. Therefore, a market area of a sari-sari store overlaps each other inside a cluster or neighborhood community, and we should think about collective market areas especially as to the cluster where many stores exist, cluster 3.

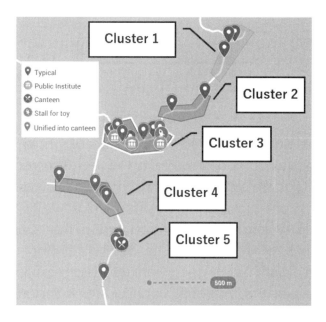

Figure 5.7. Clusters in Tagabas Ibaba

Note. Made from Google my map, retrieved from https://www.google.com/mymaps.

Figure 5.8. House-Free Areas that Separate Clusters

Note. Pictures taken by authors.

97

cluster	how many	length (m)	density (store/100m)
cluster 1	3	412	0.73
cluster 2	2	401	0.50
cluster 3	9	518	1.74
cluster 4	4	615	0.65
cluster 5	3	445	0.67

Note. Data from our research.

Table 5.9. Clusters in Tagabas Ibaba

Of the 5 clusters, cluster 3 is different from the others. There are 9 sari-sari stores out of 21 in this cluster. The store density (the number of stores per 100 meter) of the cluster 3 is 2 – 3 times larger than that of the other clusters (Table 5.9). The reason is clear, that is, the cluster 3 has the barangay hall, which has a basketball court, elementary school, and high school. Institutions gather people, and people's gathering accumulates stores.

It is natural that each market area somewhat overlaps and competes with others in a cluster, especially in cluster 3. However, for what reasons do customers chose specific sari-sari stores out of several choices? We also asked the customers why they patronized specific stores. The top reason why customers patronize specific sari-sari stores is "it is nearest" and "buying in a small unit" (called "tingi" or "takal"; 6 points) and "buying on credit" (called "utang" 5.8 points) follow (Table 5.10). On the other hand, no customer respondent chose the reasons for goods (e.g. "more inventory" or "buy goods that other stores don't sell"). Also, according to our observation and interview with owners, products that the sari-sari store sell are not differentiated.

reason	frequency				score
	1st	2nd	3rd	4th	
nearest	5	4	0	0	8.2
friendly with owner	0	0	0	6	2.4
find your friends	0	0	0	0	0
lower price	0	0	0	0	0
more inventory	0	0	0	0	0
buy goods that other don't sell	0	0	0	0	0
tingi/takal (buying in a small unit)	3	1	3	1	6
utang (buying on credit)	1	3	4	0	5.8
other	0	0	0	0	0

scores: 1st (1), 2nd (0.8), 3rd (0.6) and 4th (0.4)

Note. Data from the authers.

Table 5.10. Reason of the Patronage of Specific Sari-Sari Stores

Thus, Tagabas Ibaba as a sari-sari store market is separated into 5 clusters. Inside a cluster, each sari-sari store somewhat competes to survive, but it seems that their competition is not like a price war, nor like product differentiation. It is like differentiation on conditions around selling such as location, the way of selling and so forth, which E. Chamberlin pointed out.

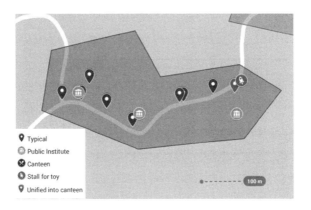

Figure 5.9. Cluster 3

Note. Made from Google my map,
Retrieved from https://www.google.com/mymaps.

Relationship Between Sari-Sari Stores and Rural Neighborhood Communities

Taking note of a communicative function of sari-sari stores, we asked the owners how many customers chat at their stores. 85.7 percent of them answered that almost all of their customers were chatting at their stores (Table 5.11). Actually, we observed customers resting and chatting at the balconies, huts, and benches of the stores. In Economics, a community is defined as a group tied with the relationship of trust formed by frequent human interaction (Hayami 1995, p.254). So, sari-sari stores there, we can think, serve as communication centers and take an important role in preserving and reproducing the human relationship in neighborhood communities.

The relationship of trust is reflected in economic activity. In Tagabas Ibaba, 100% of the owners let customers "*Utang*." *Utang* means buying on credit without interest or a contract. According to our questionnaire, *utang* sales account for 28.8 percent out of wholesales on average (Table 5.12).

choice	frequency	percentage
almost all	18	85.7%
over half	3	14.3%
over quarter	0	0%
below quarter	0	0%
sum	21	100.0%

Note. Data from the authors.

Table 5.11. Number of Customers Chat at the Sari-Sari Store

On the other hand, the more the sales of the stores depend on *utang* sales, the more sales do they earn? Table 5.13 clearly denies it. Though the larger total sales are the larger utang sales are (r=0.78, strong correlation), how high sales depend on *utang* (utang rate means sales over total sales) is irrelated to total sales (r=-0.2).

	utang/week	sales/week	utang rate
maximum	10,000	27,500	36.4%
minimum	300	1,500	20.0%
average	2,653	9,288	28.8%

Note. Data from our research.

Table 5.12. Sales as "Utang"

r	correlation between
0.78	utang SALES and total sales
-0.02	utang RATE and total sales

Table 5.13. Correlation Coefficients on Utang and Sales

The practice of *utang*, therefore, benefit consumers, especially poor ones, rather than store owner's dislike in this Barangay.

Reasons in Putting-Up or Starting Sari-Sari Stores

We asked every store owner why they start their store and why they chose a sari-sari store as a way of investment rather than other businesses. Though this is a question to an open answer, their answers are classified into only 4 patterns (Table 5.14). Almost half of the respondents (10 out of 21) answered, "because it was easy to establish and easy to manage." This includes small setup costs. Then 33.3% or 7 owners answered, "to gain extra income or to sustain daily needs." This may seem not to be the perfect answer to our intention—why did they choose especially a sari-sari store out of business choices?—but considering that there is virtually no other store-business choice in the barangay, we can think of their answers as enough reasons. 9.5% or 2 respondents said "to meet residents' needs," and interestingly, the rest of them, 2 owners, responded, "to have a hobby."

reason	number	percentage
Easy to establish and manage	10	47.6%
Extra income	7	33.3%
To meet residents' needs	2	9.5%
Hobby	2	9.5%
sum	21	100.0%

Note. Data from the questionnaire

Table 5.14. Reasons in Starting a Sari-Sari Store

Where did these owners get setup costs from? The most frequent answer to the question of where they get money from to set up the store was "from income." The second most frequent answers are "saving" and "microfinance" (Table 5.15). In spite of our expectation, no one used *Paluwagan*—a traditional rotating savings and credit association in the Philippines—, 5-6 lender—informal money lenders—, or overseas remittance when they started their stores. However, as for overseas remittance, we could find 2 owners who receive overseas remittance. One of the two uses remittance for increasing inventory as well as for daily life, education fee, and saving. The other uses remittance only for education fees and building a new house. On the other hand, none of them use *Paluwagan* for any purpose.

source of set-up cost	frequency	percentage
saving	8	30.8%
5-6 lender	0	0.0%
borrowing from relatives/friends	0	0.0%
bank	0	0.0%
paluwagan	0	0.0%
michrofinance	8	30.8%
overseas remittance	0	0.0%
income	9	34.6%
contribution in a wedding	1	3.8%
sum	26	100.0%

Note. Data from the questionnaire

Table 5.15. Source of Set-up Costs to Start Sari-Sari Store **Business**

Of the 9 owners who used income for set-up costs, 7 owners responded that they invested income from the coconut industry in setup costs. The rest of them earned income from the nurse and the catering business. As for 8 respondents who used saving to set up the stores, their income sources vary, for example, coconut industry (2), tricycle driver (2), company worker (2), construction worker (1) etc. Because coconut price is not stable, when coconut price is high, coconut formers need to invest extra profit from the high price in order to stabilize their lives. A sari-sari store easy to start should be one of the best ways for investment.

Then, how much is the set-up costs of a sari-sari store? Table 5.16 shows maximum, minimum and average setup costs. The average, 15,762 pesos, corresponds to a one-month income for a construction worker. On the other hand, the minimum, 2,000 pesos, which was invested in 2018, corresponds to 4-days income for a construction worker. Even at present, people there can start a sari-sari store with as small as 2,000 of capital.

indeces	setup costs (pesos)
maximum	100,000
minumum	2,000
average	15,762

Note. Data from the questionnaire.

Table 5.16. Set-up Costs of Sari-Sari Store

Conclusion: The Proliferation and Domination of Sari-Sari Stores

Summarizing and interpreting the results of this research, we can find the following 5 factors in sari-sari stores' domination.

First, the breakeven point for sari-sari stores should be low. The owners use their houses and their own labor force, which does not cost. Also, sari-sari stores basically sell non-perishable products such as canned goods, toiletry, snack, seasonings, and condiments. Their products can be preserved, and if some products are expiring, the owner's family can consume them, so they do not have dead stocks. Since they can go shopping both for their daily needs and for their store inventory at the same time, actual transportation costs for stocking in is limited. That's why the demand for as few as 82.9 people can support the business.

Second, people prefer the closeness of sari-sari stores. The nearer stores people want, the shorter market ranges get. The shorter market ranges are, the larger number of the stores are needed. The average market range of sari-sari stores in Tagabas Ibaba, 69 meters, is 17 meters shorter than that of convenience stores in the center of Tokyo, 86 meters if we suppose they follow traditional location theories. Closeness is the top reason why customers regularly go to specific sari-sari stores, so it differentiates a store from other stores, not in the product level, but in-store level.

Third, sari-sari stores have powerful links to neighborhood communities. Sari-sari stores provide places to communicate, and a community needs communication to sustain itself. So, we can think that neighbourhood communities naturally require sari-sari stores as communication centers.

Forth, sari-sari stores are needed by poor people, because they provide the benefit of *utang*, *tingi* and *takal* for the poor. Supermarkets or convenience stores do not provide such benefits. Actually, *tingi*, *takal* and *utang* are the second largest and third largest reasons why customers patronize sari-sari stores (Table 5.10).

Fifth, sari-sari store can be started with small capital and can be financed. Moreover, several organizations support the establishment of a sari-sari store by microfinance. Also, in coconut village like Tagabas Ibaba, a rise in coconut prices is also a cause of starting a sari-sari store.

Do these factors serve for community development? We can say "yes," mainly because the Barangay is far from the town. Of course, sari-sari stores add mark-ups to goods, but if consumers had no access to sari-sari stores, they would have to go to the town more frequently and they would be burdened with more transportation expenses. Also considering consumers' benefit from *tingi*, *takal* and *utang*, which modern retailers do not have, sari-sari stores work for improvement in the standard of the lives of the consumers, by giving the residents accessibility to goods. On the other hand, the consumers, especially women, are also potential entrepreneurs. Running a sari-sari store enables them to earn extra income and to have a more stable life by subsistence complex.

References:

Bonnin, C. (2006). "Women's Experiences as Home-Based Traders in Metro Manila: A Case Study of the Neighboorhood Sari-Sari Store," *Research and Practice in Social Sciences* 1 (2): 104-132.

Hayami, Y. (1995). *Development Economics.* Chiyoda ward, Tokyo: Sobunsha (速水佑次郎. (1995). 『開発経済学』. 創文社.).

Silverio, S. (1982). "The Neighboorhood Sari-Sari Store," in *The Philippine Poor I: Two Monographs.* Marie S. Fernandez, ed. Institute of Philippine Culture, Ateneo de Manila University.

Takemoto, R. (2016). *Japan as a Society Dependent on Convenience StoresIs Survival without Convenience Stores Impossible in the Era of Super-Aging?* Retrieved 5 24, 2019, from Discuss Japan: https://www.japanpolicyforum.jp/pdf/2016/no30/DJweb_30_soc_03.pdf.

SERVING RURAL COMMUNITIES: DECIPHERING THE ROLES OF COMMUNITY BUSINESS IN PROVIDING BASIC GOODS AND SERVICES TO RURAL COMMUNITIES

CONSTANTINE BUSUNGU[1] AND DELPHINE KESSY[1]

1 Department of Tourism and Hospitality Management
St.Augustine University of Tanzania

Introduction

Stakeholders and Governments in developing countries, particularly those in Sub-Saharan Africa have now come to the recognition that economic development will only be fruitful if the poorest rural communities will be integrated into the development agenda. The incorporation of rural areas and rural communities in development agenda brought forward out of the reality that rural people comprises a significant portion of the population in developing countries and it is estimated that the majority of the poor are projected to continue to live in rural areas until 2040 (Maxwell *et al.*, 2001; Ravallion *et al.*, 2007).

According to (UN, 2018) during the period from 1950 to 2017, the rural population of less-developed countries increased from 1.4 billion to over 4 billion with most of these increases coming from Africa and Asia. This demographic swing has had substantial effects on rural-development dynamics. In some instances, rural population growth meant a positive shift in development inspiring technological progress or allowing economies of scale in production and infrastructure and thus opened the way to rural economic growth, which in turn has led to declines in mortality and fertility levels in accordance with the familiar concept of demographic transition. Whereas in some examples rural population growth resulted in negative effects in rural development including increased job insecurity, misery, crimes and environmental degradations (Anríquez, 2007; Anríquez and Stloukal, 2008).

The United Republic of Tanzania is the second-largest economy in the East African Community and the twelfth largest in Africa. Tanzania, like other developing countries, has a large rural population: More than 67 percent of the total population lives in rural areas and depends on agriculture and agriculture-related activities as their primary employment and source of food. In 2016 the rural population increased to 37,613,490 as compared to 9,545,998 after Tanzania independence in 1960 (World Bank, 2007a, Chongela, 2015; Page, 2016; Davis *et al.*, 2017).

Rural development in Tanzania holds huge potential for transforming people's livelihoods, economic growth and poverty eradication given that in Tanzania more than 60% of the population resides in rural areas and small towns. Since its independence, the United Republic of Tanzania through different phases of government has tried different strategies to bring about change and economic development and throughout these phases, the rural sectors have been the keystone of the country's development strategy. For the socio-economic development of Tanzania, agriculture is almost everything and keeping in mind that no country has significantly reduced the poverty of its population without achieving a high level of productivity in agriculture (Grewal *et al.*, 2012; Pingali, 2012 ;). Tanzania has in the past implemented a number of initiatives in an effort to unleash its agricultural potential including villagization program in 1971-1973, *siasa ni kilimo* (politics is agriculture) in 1974, *kilimo cha kufa na kupona* (produce or perish philosophy) in 1974-1975, *kilimo kwanza* (agriculture first initiatives) in 2009, big results now (BRN) in 2013/2014 and currently the fifth phase government of Tanzania is implementing second agricultural sector development program (ASDP II) costing a total of $5.9 billion dollars for ten years starting in 2017/2018 (IFPRI 2000; Isinika *et al*, 2005; Therkildsen, 2011; URT 2016).

The principal aim of this paper is to provide some insights into the role and types of community businesses in fostering the development and revitalization in rural Tanzania. The specific objectives of this study are the following: (1) to identify the major constraints to rural development; (2) to identify and describe the types of community business   practices in rural Tanzania; (3) To determine the contribution of community business in serving rural communities; (4) To   determine the role of community business in employing of   rural youth and balancing rural youth out-migration and (5) to draw some lessons from Tanzania's experience in rural community business which may be useful for future policy action in Tanzania, as well as for rural development in Africa.

Problem Statement and Justification of the Study

There have been numerous efforts and strategies by Tanzania government, donors and other development stakeholders to promote development particularly, rural areas. There have been some success stories but the majority of rural areas are in a poor state and most rural economies are weak and upsetting. The rural areas in Tanzania have typical problems which include poor living standards, low income, low productivity, and high level of unemployment, high population rate, poor technological growth, poor infrastructure, high illiteracy rate, and malnutrition. According to Steiner and Atterton (2014); Steiner and Markantoni (2013) entrepreneurship and community business activities play a vital role in influencing the livelihoods and resilience of rural communities in direct and indirect ways and both are important in shaping the resilience of rural places. Community business can help reduce the problem of employment, deliver basic services and products to rural communities, keep scarce resources within the community as well as contribute to the rural community capability to sustain itself in the course of change through adaptation and sporadic transformation. Yet, little information has been documented or analyzed with regards to the role and potential of community business in accelerating economic development and transforming the rural communities in Tanzania. Establishment of appropriate rural development strategies or policies cannot be guaranteed unless there is sufficient knowledge on the role and potential of community business. Consequently, the focal point of this study was to decipher the roles of community businesses in providing basic goods and services to rural communities.

Literature Review:

Rural Areas

Varieties of definitions are used to describe rural areas. Each definition emphasizes different criteria and among those criteria includes population size, density, context, and distance or accessibility to urban centers are the two most common criteria used to determine the nature and extent of rural areas. According to Statistics Canada (1999a) and rural area is defined as a sparsely populated geographic area that is located outside urban areas. Each variation of definition can create a different view about rural people but in the final analysis, rural people have similar characteristics. Among the common features that characterize the rural people include low employment rate, lower-income and dependency on agriculture (Statistics Canada 1999a, Maxwell, et al., 2001).

Rural-rural Linkages

Rural people are not entirely isolated; isolation can be conceptualized in terms of distance from urban areas, poor infrastructure and social services inadequacy, distance from an economic nucleus or distance from political decision making (Bird et al., 2010). With all due respect of interdependence between rural and urban communities, there exists another interaction between one rural community with another rural community (Burholt and Naylor, 2005). The interactions between rural communities are vital in supplying the community needs and keeping the quest and hope for future development alive.

Rural-urban Linkages

Rural-urban linkages are defined movement of materials across space as well as movement between that occur from rural to urban and from urban to rural areas. Movement of materials across space entails the flow of people, commodities, wealth, know-how, knowledge, waste, information and services. Meanwhile, the movement of material between sectors involves movement of agricultural produces and raw material from rural to urban areas, and movement of manufactured or imported goods from urban to rural areas (Bah *et al.*, 2003; AAH, 2012). The rural-urban linkages are usually depicted in the nature and forms of migration, production, consumption, financial and some investment linkages that occur within the rural-urban symbiosis. The benefits that can be gained in taking the rural-urban approach to policy development as the future includes the exchange of cash, commodities, tourists which might involve socio-cultural activities and communication with friends and relatives might be used as indicators of a healthy rural -urban linkage. These links are not only key components of livelihoods and of local economies; they are also 'engines' that drive economic, social and cultural transformations for both rural and urban areas. The dynamic shifts in rural-urban linkages have the potential to affect the livelihoods of low-income and vulnerable groups in both urban and rural settlements. Despite the difference in activities, economies of scales and opportunities studies of rural-urban linkages seek to augment the generation of more inclusive development policies for both rural and urban inhabitants. Indeed, there are rural economies that are heavily dependent on focusing on the interdependencies and commonalities rather than on differences. Likewise, our common (rural and urban) success depends on our ability to make constructive use of these interdependencies and on encouraging rural-urban linkages that bridge the divides across economic geography.

Lewis model and Rural-urban Interaction

According to Lewis model (1954), the growth of a developing economy needs surplus labor transfer between two sectors, the capitalist sector (mostly, urban non-agricultural and industrial) and the subsistence sector (mostly rural and agricultural). The model is sometimes referred to as `dual' economies, conceived of as economies with both an industrial sector and a rural sector. The Lewis model helped to explain the economic development of European countries through the reallocation of labor from the subsistence sector to the capitalist sector after the industrial revolution in the 1800s (Timmer, 1988; Boianovsky, 2017). In addition, this model illuminates pathways of some latest success stories of countries like South Korea, China, Singapore, Taiwan and India which were poor countries prior to the 1950s but were able to industrialize and achieved generally rising living standards (Timmer, 1988; Kay, 2009). Unpredictable weather conditions and droughts imply significant income risk to Tanzanian households engaged in agriculture (Kinda and Leoning, 2010). Therefore, the application of the Lewis model of shifting from the subsistence sector which is mainly agricultural to the capital sector which is mainly non-agricultural would be worthwhile.

Brick and Mortar Model

A Brick and Mortar business model is the conventional business model that uses the traditional channels of delivering value. Many consumers still prefer to shop and browse in a physical store and this is because in brick-and-mortar consumers can speak, ask questions about products or services and use all their senses to touch, see, try and take the product home immediately

According to Amankwah-Amoah (2017) in the 21st century will persist especially social-orientated countries mainly because of the seller-buyer (customer interaction as good are showcased on shops or market). The customers or consumer have a chance to use all their senses therefore when there is a product-customer mismatch, the customer can get assistance to find products which will bring utility. Under this model, the customer buying behavior can be known and analyzed. In spite of the fact that the Brick and Mortar business model consumes much time in comparison to the modern model, people worldwide still prefer this model. Some of the advantages of Brick and Mortar business models as acknowledged by (Enders & Jelassi, 2000) are easy to establish a brand name, wider customer base, sense of security, an intimate relationship between customer and seller and amazing shopping experience of the customer. Community businesses such as *maduka* and *gulio* emphasize interaction and social networks in the community where they are established. Using Brick and Mortar business models for rural communities is likely to resonate with the rural people because of not only satisfaction but also interaction and social networks which are key elements for rural life.

Community Business

Rural communities in Tanzania are searching for ways to reinforce their economies, endow with better living standards, build local assets and prevent rapid rural out migrations. The most helpful and enviable economic development strategy for many rural communities is community business. Community businesses in Tanzania are characterized in the form of shops that sells virtually everything in retails " (ma)duka" in the plural and "duka" in the singular, vendor stalls "(ma)genge", weekly organizer bazaar "(ma)gulio" and other forms. These businesses have been proven to work in rural areas that have not been successful in attracting manufacturers or other large employers from outside. Community businesses are especially important these days, as opportunities shrivel to attract large employers to distant rural areas. Companies that formerly looked to rural communities for cheap labor are now moving offshore for even lower-wage labor. There are also social advantages to develop strategies based on community business. It keeps profits in the community. It creates a mix of opportunities. Community business creates some low wage jobs, but it also provides significant numbers of opportunities for people to build assets and earn middle-class incomes as business owners. In an era when real wages are falling in many industries, creating a chance for people who work to be business owners creates more equality and opportunity. Finally, nurturing locally owned businesses puts the economic future of the community in the hands of its own members – people committed to its future (Johnstone and Lionais 2004).

According to McKenzie et al (2014), developing countries should be interested in community business and small rural entrepreneurship because they represent a large share of firms and development in these countries. Tulus, Tahi, Hamonangan & Tambunan (2011) pointed out that small and medium community businesses are not only vital because they are a source of employment but also because they are a source of efficiency, growth and economic decentralization.

(Ma) Gulio

The term *magulio* for plural and *gulio* for singular in the Swahili language represents a weekly organized open market in Tanzania. An open market is an economic system with no barriers to free-market activity. Anyone can participate in an open market, which is characterized by the absence of tariffs, taxes, licensing requirements, subsidies, unionization, and any other regulations or practices that interfere with naturally functioning operations. Open markets may have competitive barriers to entry, but never any regulatory barriers to entry.

In rural Tanzania, *gulio* is one of the major economic activities. Space or location where the *gulio* is done is composed of temporary structures and it is determined by the local government in consultations with the local communities. The rural communities, traders and middlemen bring their goods and services at the *gulio*. The rural communities' products mostly are semi-processed and agricultural-based such as rice, vegetables, maize, chicken, yogurt and tobacco. The traders are mostly small scale petty traders who brings products which are industrial goods like cloth, domestic utensils, electronics while middlemen bring either agricultural products or industrial products. Other services like food and drinks are served in temporary structures such as booths and *magenge*. In an open market, the pricing of goods or services is driven predominantly by the principles of supply and demand with limited interference or outside influence from large conglomerates or governmental agencies.

Gulio in rural settings is looked upon as an area of showcasing community business, a source for new venture creation and growth in existing businesses in rural communities. The increase of importance of *gulio* can propel the revival of strong and sustainable community business and help in exploring new types of services to support rural communities. This, in turn, will help to boost rural employment, income, and development of rural areas (Baumgartner *et al*, 2013, Ferris *et al.*, 2014). A good function *gulio* in Tanzania is the health indicators of economic prosperity, strong community business, and rural resilience.

There are regrettably few lucid studies on the socio-economic and political significance of *magulio* in Tanzania. This is a pioneer study in *magulio* and it emphasizes the extensive study of *magulio* because of their significance and the role they particularly play in rural development in Tanzania.

Conceptual framework for Community Business Model

The purpose of this section is to present a conceptual framework that is general and flexible in understanding variables related to community businesses and their impacts on communities in rural areas and small towns. At any time, the meaning, variables, and understanding of the rural environment are crucial in framing strategies for sustainable community businesses and rural development (Zaridis and Mousiolis, 2014).

A variable is an element, feature or factor and is liable to vary or change. This research has focused on three variables as shown in the conceptual model. From the Conceptual Framework below, the Independent variables are the factor that manipulates (i.e. changes) and therefore is assumed to have a direct effect on the dependent variable. Dependent variables are the factors that are assumed to change or influenced by independent variables while intervening variable hypothetically used to explain causal links between other variables i.e. independent and dependent variable (Kothari, 2004).

At any time in small towns and rural areas of Tanzania, the community businesses is a multidimensional process. In considering this framework, we emphasize the movement of materials, goods, and services from either urban to rural, rural to urban or rural to rural. The materials, goods, and services are different in each direction, function as well, utility to the end-users. The perspective from our study indicates that in order for community businesses to strive, it has to be flexible and highly adaptable. In addition to that mutual collaboration and networking can help rural community businesses to absorb changes, learn and develop, and respond to changes in the business environment.

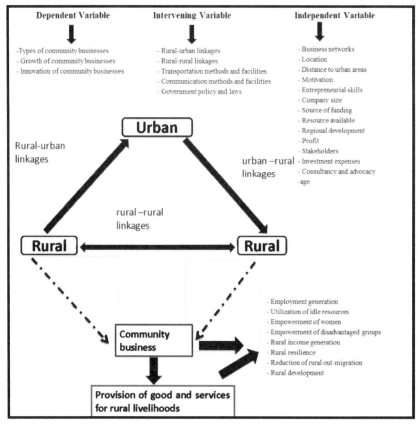

Figure 6.1. Independent and Dependent Variable in Community Business Model
Source (Authors Visualization based on field condition)

Methodologies:

Study areas

The study area comprises Usagara and Nyang'holongo village in the Misungwi district located in the Mwanza region. They display homogenous, environmental, and agro-climatic characteristics and both are rural areas that have a high emergence of community business. While the weekly organizer bazaar or *gulio* in Usagara is conducted on Saturday, the *gulio* in Nyang'holongo is conducted on Sunday. These villages are located between latitudes 2.63° and 2.72° south of the equator and longitudes 32.99 and 33.11° respectively with an elevation of 1301m below sea level. According to the Tanzania Census (2012), these villages had a population of 1820 and 3215 for Nyang'holongo and Usagara respectively.

Design and Sampling

A mixed research method approach was used to capture both quantitative and qualitative data from the study area. The idea of integrating qualitative and quantitative approaches is to maintain the strengths meanwhile, reducing the weaknesses in both approaches (Bergman, 2009b). In this study, primary data was collected using a questionnaire and focus group discussions. This study used a purposive sampling strategy. The purposive sampling involves identifying and selecting individuals or groups of individuals that are especially knowledgeable about or experienced with a phenomenon of interest (Cresswell and Plano, 2011). In this study, the researcher selected respondents that were deemed to have in-depth knowledge about community business. Secondary data were collected at village government offices. Statistical Package for Social Sciences (SPSS) was used for quantitative data analysis. Descriptive and content analysis was adopted for qualitative data.

Results:

Demographic Characteristics of Community Business owners

In the present study, it was found that there were a high number of male owning community businesses compared to the female. There were 218 male business owners which make 66% of the total community business owners and 111female business owners making a total of 34% of the total business owners in Usagara and Nyang'holongo villages (Table 6.1).

Table 6.1 indicates the community business owner's variation in their ages and therefore was categorized into 4 major groups. The first group is composed of a community whose age falls below the age of 20. The second group is for the community whose age falls between 20 and 35 years old. The third group is those community whose age falls between 36 and 55 years of age and the fourth group is the community falls above 55 years of age. Few business owners belonged to below 20 and above 55 of age. Both were only 41 people equivalent to 12.2% for each age category. While the age category of 20-35 and 36-55 had a high number of business owners which were 127(38.6%) and 122(37%) respectively.

Education and business training at any level has the ability to strengthen people' entrepreneurial knowledge hence influencing the opening and operation of community businesses. In the present study, it was found that level of education of the majority of community business owners 167 (50.6%) had attained primary school education while business owners with secondary education were 97(29.4%) had a secondary school education, 45(13.6%) had a college education and 21 (6.4%) had not attended any formal education (Table 6.1).

Marital status is a critical variable in determining the level and magnitude of conflict arising from the inheritance of land or wealth, gender equality and equal access to opportunities and wealth. Married women, for instance, have the burden of domestic activities and sometimes they don't have freedom like their single, divorced and widowed counterparts. Therefore this can affect their chance to participate in the community business. In this study, a large percentage of business owners 113 (34.3%) were married, 79 (24%) were cohabitating. 76(23) were singles, 31 (9.4) were divorced and the same number again 31(6.4%) were widowed (Table 6.1).

Community Businesses	Age group				Gender		Level of education				Marital status					Total
	<20	21-35	36-55	>55	M	F	No	P	S	C	Ma	Si	Di	Wi	Co	
Maduka	26	54	86	33	142	57	10	96	61	32	72	30	26	19	52	199
Magenge	4	34	5	0	10	33	2	31	10	0	8	24	2	4	5	43
Restaurants	2	10	5	0	15	2	5	8	4	0	3	5	2	1	6	17
Liquor shops	3	7	2	1	9	4	1	6	4	2	6	3	0	1	3	13
Barber shops	4	9	1	0	14	0	2	5	4	3	2	7	0	0	5	14
Butchers	0	0	4	0	4	0	0	4	0	0	3	0	0	1	0	4
Hair saloons	1	4	2	0	0	6	0	2	2	2	2	3	0	0	1	6
Electrionic shops	0	0	4	2	5	1	0	3	2	1	4	0	0	1	1	6
Cloth shop	1	4	2	1	4	4	0	4	3	1	4	1	0	1	2	8
Building materials	0	0	5	2	7	0	0	3	3	1	4	0	0	1	2	7
Others	0	5	6	2	8	4	1	5	4	3	5	3	1	2	2	13
Total	41	127	122	41	218	111	21	167	97	45	113	76	31	31	79	330
Percentage(%)	12.2	38.6	37.0	12.2	66.0	44.0	6.4	50.6	29.4	13.6	34.3	23.0	9.4	9.4	24.0	100

Table 6.1. Demographic Characteristics of Respondents (n=330)

*Letter M and F represents Male and Female respectively
* Symbol No represent owners of community business with no education while letter P, S and C represents Primary school education, Secondary school and College/University education respectively
*Symbol Ma, Si, Wi, and Co represents married, single, divorced and cohabitation respectively.

Community Businesses

Community business is the most recent research discipline in the entrepreneurship field. Community businesses involve all types of businesses that are operated in the community for the purpose of giving products and services to the community in question. Community businesses in Tanzania are characterized in the form of shops that sells virtually everything in retails *"maduka"*, vendor stalls *"magenge"*, weekly organizer open market *"gulio"* and other forms. The current study a number of community businesses in Usagara and Nyang'holongo villages and is presented in Fig. 6.1 and Fig. 6.2 for Usagara and Nyang'holongo respectively. The highest numbers of community businesses were *maduka* which had a total number of 199 among them 136 in Usagara and 63 in Nyang'holongo. The ma (duka) has two types: first is *duka la jumla* (wholesale duka) this sells goods in large amounts and the second one is duka la *reja reja* (retail duka) who sales good in small quantities. The wholesale duka owner sells goods to retail duka owners in a relation herein described as business to business (B2B) relationship while the retail duka owners, they usually sell the products to consumers in a relationship herein described as business to consumer (B2C) relationship.

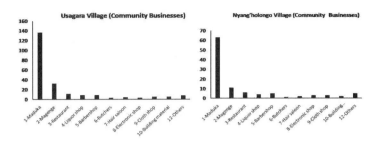

Figure 6.2. Community businesses in Usagara village.
Figure 6.3. Community business in Nyang'holongo village.

The second community businesses with higher numbers were Magenge which were 43 among them 32 in Usagara and 11 in Nyang'holongo. The third community business with a higher number were restaurants which were 17 community businesses and among them 11 in Usagara and 6 in Nyang'holongo. Other community businesses included liquor shops (13), barber shops (14), cloth shop(8), building materials hardware(7), hair salons(6), electronic shops (6), butchers(4) and others(13). The other community business included wood shops, tailors, shoe shops, craft shops, charcoal shops, bars, and guest houses. All these help in providing necessary goods and services on a daily basis to the community.

Typical liquor shop and Hair beauty saloon (for women only)

Genge (Selling Partially Processed Agricultural Products Mainly from Rural Areas)

Gulio (Industrial Goods Mainly brought from Urban Areas)

Barbershops (for men and women)

126

Duka

Source of Funding of Community Businesses

Developed countries have friendly financial and bank policies therefore it is often easy to raise funding or capital for a startup business or for expanding their businesses into new markets or locations. Contrary to that in developing countries like Tanzania, particularly in rural areas, the financial /bank policies are not favorable and little support is given by the government for starting a business. The source of funding mostly comes from savings obtained from agricultural related activities (Kinda and Loening 2010).

Therefore, the source of funding remains a critical variable that can determine either positively or negatively the growth and success of community businesses in the rural areas of Tanzania. In the study areas, it was found that about 155(47%) business owners had their funding or startup derived from their personal savings, 63(19%) from Savings and Credit Co-operative Societies (SACCOS), 26 (8%) from family or friends, 23(7%) from banks, 30 (9%) from

127

other sources, 20 (6%) from contract with other companies or businesses and 13 (4%) had inherited the community business from parent, husbands or wife. The breakdown of the finding is summarized in Table 2.

Source of Funding	Number of Community Business	Percentage of Community Business
Personal saving	155	47%
Bank loans	23	7%
SACCOS	63	19%
Family and friends	26	8%
Successions	13	4%
Contract-based (malikauli)	20	6%
Others	30	9%
Total	330	100%

Table 6.2: Source of funding of Community Businesses in Usagara and Nyang'holongo villages

Community Served (Customers)

Customers represent an individual person or a company that purchases goods and services from another business company. In this study, the customer represents all the people and company that purchases goods and services from the community businesses in Usagara and Nyang'holongo villages. The interviews and focused group discussion study revealed that 64% of the customers in community business were indigenous community members, 24% were from neighboring villages, 10% of the customers were transit customers that stayed for few hours in the area of study while 5% of the customers were from Mwanza city. These findings are illustrated in Fig. 6.4.

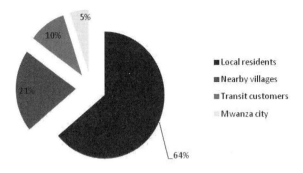

Figure 6.4. Customers for Community Businesses in Usagara and Nyang'holongo villages

Source of Goods and Services

Goods and services are items that are sold by community businesses. Goods and services can be either tangible such as salt, sugar, and mangoes or intangible such as barbers, waiters or digital services. According to economic theory consumption of goods and services, it is assumed to provide utility or satisfaction to the customer or end-user. Sources of goods and services offered are vital in determining the level of development and balance payment of the given area of study. In this study, 54% of goods and services offered or sold by community business has their origin in Mwanza city, 30% have their origin in the study area, 10% have their origin from the nearby village and 6% have their origin from other numerous places.

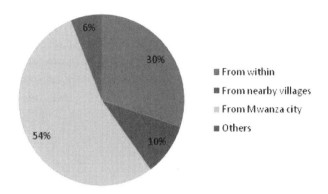

Figure 6.5. Sources of Goods and Services
Sold by Community Businesses In Usagara and Nyang'holongo Villages

The Seasonality of sales volume for Community Businesses

Community businesses are prone to seasonality like any other business. Seasonality is any predictable fluctuation or pattern of sales volume of goods or services from businesses enterprise that recurs or repeats over a year. Conceivably, the utmost advantage to understanding how seasonality affects business sales is it gives clues to business owners into what they can and can not control hence sometimes sales will be down and sometimes will be up Seasonality is a trademark of the Tanzanian rural non-agricultural sector especially community businesses, a variation principally owing to labor supply, demand for rural products, and availability of raw materials which all depend on the agricultural sector. The findings from our study showed that the month of June had the highest sales volume with a sales volume percentage of 25 followed by December, May, April, and July. The sales volume in November, October, September, August and March had medium to low sales volume while February and January had the lowest sales volume for community business. The finding of the seasonality of sales volume of goods and services from community businesses is summarized in Fig. 6.6.

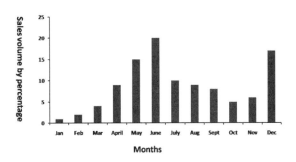

Figure 6.6. Seasonality of Sales Volume of Goods and Services from Community Businesses

Gulio versus other Community Businesses

In rural Tanzania, *gulio* is one of the major economic activities. Although is weekly organized, it represents a high opportunity for rural community businesses to sell, showcase their products and services, higher interaction with customers, the establishment of business networks and learn from other companies. We analyzed the utility/ satisfaction level of *gulio* in rural and urban areas and compared it with the utility/satisfaction level with that of other community businesses.

The result indicates that although shops (*maduka*) represent a large percentage of community businesses (199) out of 330 community businesses in Usagara and Nyang'holongo villages (Fig. 6.2 and Fig 6.3), it is from *gulio* that the community gets more satisfaction and buys more volumes of goods and services per day. Unlike in rural areas, *maduka* represents a more convenient in urban areas, more affordable, user-friendly and cheapest way of getting goods and services. Despite this, in both rural and urban areas the presence of *gulio* and other community businesses can complement each other. The diagram below depicts the relationship between *gulio* and other community businesses in rural and urban areas.

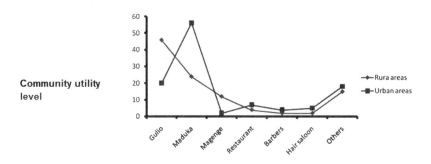

Figure 6.7. Rural and Urban utility level of gulio versus Other Community Businesses

Perception of Community Businesses

Community businesses are considered to be a significant tool for unleashing the potentials of the marginalized and deprived rural communities ties isolated from the mainstream economy and is important in bringing social upliftment for youth, middle-aged, women's and gender equity as well as rural resilience. In this study, 63.8 percent of the respondents thought or believed that community business had a very high (23.3%) and high (40%) contribution to the sustainable development of Usagara and Nyang'holongo villages. Whereas very few respondents (8.8%) thought or believed that community business had minimal contribution towards sustainable development. 27.5% of the respondents had the perception that the contribution of community business to sustainable development had a moderate impact. The finding on the perception of community business to sustainable development is summarized in Table 6.3.

Contribution of community business	Number of individuals	Percentage
very high	79	23.8
high	132	40.0
moderate	91	27.5
low	21	6.3
very low	8	2.5
Total	330	100.0

Table 6.3. Perceptions of the Contribution of Community Business to Rural Sustainable Development

Usagara and Nyang'holongo village's Population Dynamics

The population change and dynamics have effects on the business and hence economic growth of an area or country. According to Thuku (2013), three theories explain the relationship between population growth and economic growth. The first theory explains that population growth stimulates economic growth. The second theory visualizes population growth as a hindrance or obstacle in achieving economic growth whereas the third theory states that population growth is a neutral factor in economic growth and is determined outside standard growth models. In the present research study, we found that the number of households and population of Usagara and Nyang'holongo villages were increasing at a pace similar to that of national demographic estimates (URT, 2013) the findings are summarized in Table 6.4.

	Usagara		Nyang'holongo	
	Households	Population	Households	Population
2002 (Census)	161	972	129	784
2012 (Census)	590	3215	365	1820
2019 (VEO data)	1218	5639	644	2947

Table 6.4. Usagara and Nyang'holongo village Population Dynamics

Discussion

The findings from this research suggest that community businesses are paramount in providing rural communities with necessary goods and services for everyday needs. Also, community businesses enhance economies, vitality, and resilience of rural communities. In the current study, we found that business networks, the location of the community business, distance to urban areas, source of funding, resources available, consultancy, age, level of education, gender and age were the key variables that are influencing establishment and success of community businesses in Usagara and Nyang'holongo villages. Moreover, at any time rural-urban linkages, rural-rural linkages, transportation methods facilities, communication methods and facilities, government policy and laws were the causal links between other variables. We will discuss the findings of this study in terms of their theoretical and practical implications and suggest directions for future research in community businesses.

The philosophy that agriculture contributes to structural transformation pioneered by Lewis (1954), postulated that economic development comes as a result of relocating factors of production from an agricultural sector characterized by low productivity and the use of traditional techniques to a modern industrial sector with higher productivity. This theory was adopted by many developing countries at that time such as South Korea, Taiwan, China, and India in the 1950s and 1960s which resulted in sustained development (Lele and Mellor, 1981). Ranis (2004) suggested that this theory is still pertinent these days and plays a vital role as a policy guide for labor-abundant countries with high population pressure and scarcity of cultivable land. There is also a historical verification for the applicability of this model for some countries such as England (1780-1840), Japan (1870-1920) and Taiwan (1980-1970) which they realized economic growth as a result of surplus labor moving to urban areas (Smitka, 1998; Ranis, 2004).

Our study found the rural population of Usagara and Nyang'holongo villages was increasing at a rate of (3.1 per year). The average household size of 5-8 people per house and the increase of population are consistent with Tanzania 2012 census (URT, 2013). This indicates the population growth rate has not changed, especially in rural areas where issues of family planning are rarely practiced. However, the increase of population does not necessarily mean there is zero rural out-migration. We found out that people, especially educated young people, are moving to urban areas to find high paying technical jobs but at the same time, there is evidence of people (middle-aged and old people) from Mwanza city shifting to rural areas especially Usagara village. Despite the lack of clear connection of surplus labor migration from our study areas to urban, this model is still applicable in Tanzania and Africa as well, particularly where the urban areas are highly industrialized and the rural areas with the largest percentage of households are limited to the agriculture sector.

Despite the fact that in developing countries, a large percent of the population lives in rural areas (UN 2018). The attention of studies on community business and entrepreneurship in Africa has been given to urban areas (Alemu and Adesina 2017; Naude, 2011). According to Lewis (1954), the rural economy was anticipated to become less significant as a contributor to rural household income over time (Lanjouw and Lanjouw, 2001). This study, however, found that the community businesses in rural areas are the major source of income, economic activities, employment, and innovation. The rural community businesses are enhancing people's livelihoods, revitalizing rural life and giving resilience to stay in rural areas and fight for their life rather than taking the risk to migrate to urban areas where life might be unpredictable.

This study tried to highlight the development of an all-inclusive approach towards community businesses that can augment livelihood in rural areas and small towns. It is obvious that community businesses in the study areas were results of push-pull factors that were motivated by community needs and undertaken with the prospect of using rural resources and opportunities to get profits that can be used for the betterment and prosperity of the whole community. However, it was noted in this study that most of the industrial products and services that were being sold by these communities were from urban (Mwanza City) implying few small industries in rural areas as well as high dependency on urban areas. This implies that rural communities cannot provide all the basic goods and services to its inhabitants. Hence, they tend to depend on each other for economic products. This interaction between rural and urban areas enhances rural community business diversification and thriving of economic activities in the rural area and small towns and hence the rural areas can no longer be ignored as economic deadwood but need to be seen as investment frontiers for a wide range of businesses in the community (Jarvis and Dunham 2003). There is a need for the government and all development stakeholders to devise a way of promoting and strengthening the existing capacities for small scale industries in rural areas and small towns. The fact that community businesses serve 64 percent of the community needs and 24 percent of nearby village needs entails how significant role it played in serving goods and services to rural people and more effort should be done to improve the business environment so that more businesses that cater every facet of community needs. Communities are stronger when more people working on farms and businesses have the opportunity to own them.

Businesses use different models to appeal and reach their customers (Osterwalder and Pigneur, 2010). It is undoubtedly technology in the 21st century that has changed the way people do shopping. According to Gallaugher (2002); Steinfield et al., (2002) people use technologies to search for information on a product online, purchase goods, and compare prices. Unlike in urban areas and cities where internet facilities are good in rural areas community businesses usually use traditional models such as the Brick and Mortar model. Brick and Mortar Business Model refer a traditional business model that uses the customary channels to capture and deliver value to the customers. According to Enders and Jelassi, (2000), "Thc Bricks and Mortar model of retailing is based on physical shops where the seller and customer interact and build a relationship." Under this model, the goods and services are displayed in the shops where the customers can use all their senses to touch, see, try and take the product or use the service. The observed business model in Usagara and Nyang'holongo villages resembles a Bricks and Mortar model which stresses the use of all senses and social interaction. The interaction between buyer and seller in the community goes beyond just selling and buying as in most cases the buyer and seller they know each other and they make stories talk about social issues and events in the community even before the act of buying and selling.

This study revealed that a community business in Usagara and Nyang'holongo villages is dominated by shops "(ma)duka"(60%), followed by vendor stalls "magenge" (14%), restaurants (4.5%), liquor shops (5%), butchers (0.5%), saloons (1%), electronic shop (2%) hardware(1%) cloth shop (3%), barbershops (5%) and others (4%). However, rural people get the utmost satisfaction through the weekly organized bazaar "*gulio*". In contrast to rural areas shops " (ma) duka" is very important in urban areas and represent the utmost satisfaction to urban communities. The importance of weekly organized bazaar "*gulio*" in rural areas is because of several factors including availability of a wide range of products and services, cheapest price, high chance of offers and natural environment which permits high interaction and leisure for the rural people. In urban areas shops "(ma)duka" are more favored due to convenience, chance to pay in installment or debt and close relationship between the "(ma)duka" owners and urban dwellers. Similarly, it was noted that connectivity in the form of telecommunication, infrastructure, and transportation is a key variable that drives community businesses to achieve success and contribute more to the rural community.

Community business prosperity is the most important goal of every business. Therefore, it is very imperative to spot out the factors that guide the success of the business. The literature has confirmed the impact of several demographic characteristics on business prosperity. Many studies have highlighted the role of demographic characteristics such as age, religion, gender, experience, background, and education of entrepreneurs towards their entrepreneurial behaviors and firm's performance (Wiklund and Shepherd 2003; Chow, 2006). In this study, we examined some characteristics of community business owners. For instance, we found that most of the owners of community businesses are middle-aged between the late twenties to fifty. This suggests that young people are prone to rural-urban migration and are not yet settled enough to perform in business while the older people beyond sixty years of age cannot handle the everyday hassling involved in community businesses. The age of community business owners is an important personal characteristic that influences the development and maintenance of businesses. Gender was another demographic characteristic that was checked in this study and results show 66% of men versus 44% of women owning community business. Apparently, it was clear that some community businesses were owned by women alone, the whole other were for men, for instance, barbershops, butchery and building material stores were men-owned whereas beauty hair saloon was owned by women. Ma(duka) were dominated by men while restaurants and Magenge were dominated by women owners. The imbalance of gender highlighted here but in other villages, the situation might be worse than in Usagara and Nyang'holongo villages. Some literature suggests businesses, especially women-owned, are prone to difficulty in getting credit from formal sources (Berger and Udell 2006). Likewise, other researches remarks that women-owned businesses have lower loan approval rates from formal sources indicating credit market discrimination (Muravyev *et al.*, 2009). Therefore, it is argued that community business is important areas where women in rural and small communities have a chance to excel so they have to be supported, encouraged and empowered to attain economic success and security. In other words, self-employment and entrepreneurship may be desirable options to these women in light of the opportunities available in rural labor markets.

The research has also shown that a combination of marital statuses such as married, single, cohabitation and divorces have significant effects on community business' success and owner's earnings during our study. This agrees to Loscocco and Leicht (1993), which in turn affects the sustainability of households. One of the contributing factors is that managers who are married spend more time on domestic duties and are therefore more likely to generate proportionately lower earnings from their businesses. One characteristic of the rural hinterland is the predominance of family and traditional gender roles, compared to urban centers. As noted above, this may limit the ability of women to run their own businesses.

Similarly, the education levels of business owners can influence community business' success and earnings. According to Bosire and Etyang (2003) on studies conducted in Kenya, those individuals that have better training, starting from secondary education, acquire specific and technical knowledge which improve their capabilities to facilitate personal development in certain professions and help them start entrepreneurial activities where they may be put into practices. This agrees with Pathak et al., (2013) who conducted research on the impact of education in women business owners whereas (Urban, 2004) pointed that psychological variables and race and ethnicity area is important as education in determining business performance and entrepreneurial activity. In our study, we found about 50% of community business owners had primary education. 29% secondary education, 14 % college education and 7 % had only informal education. It was noted that simple community businesses which do not involve complex decision making and planning like restaurants and *magenge* were owned by owners with lower education level while complex community businesses which require complex decision making, planning and, innovation were owned by people with a high level of education such as secondary and college education.

Furthermore, the study looked at the seasonality of doing businesses by comparing the volume of sales between months of community businesses. The results show that the month of June had the highest sales volume followed in December while January and February had the lowest sales volume. The highest sales months start from April and its end in around August, it picks again in December. This pattern of sales coincides with months with a high harvest with just the exception of the months of December. This suggests that most rural people still depend highly on the agricultural sector for their income. The spending or buying of goods and services from community business increases just after start getting harvest from their agricultural production. In some years where the agricultural production is lower due to low rainfall the net spend /buying of goods and services from community business are lower as well. Efforts should be made by the government and development partners to help rural communities to reduce dependence on the agricultural sector and shift some of the burdens to non-agricultural sectors such as tourism and manufacturing. This will boost the rural economy, reduce the seasonality of sales and increase the chance of community business success.

Eventually, the study looked at various challenges the community businesses and business owners face in their daily activities. We uncovered some interesting aspects of the daily life of community businesses including the formalizing process of the community business whereby this process is coupled with bureaucracy and corruption. Secondly, challenges emanating from start-up capital and bank loans as you can see (Table 2) most of the startup is from personal savings, SACCOS and from family and relatives. The banks' conditions are very difficult and interest rates are very high and many community businesses fail to meet the condition or fail to repay back the loans and in most cases when a community business owner takes a bank loan it leads to bankruptcy. Thirdly, there are few chances of training or any government incentives to business owners which can keep these businesses on track and successful. Nevertheless, there are still some constraints to growth and significantly amongst these are intense competition, so many taxes from government and dealing with corruption amongst regulatory officials.

Acknowledgment

The authors wish to express heartfelt appreciation to Mr. Cazmiry Z. Chai (Usagara Ward Executive Officer), Ms. Anna Obunga Juma (Usagara Village Executive Officer), Mr. Abas Alfred Allex (Assistant at Usagara Village Officer) and Ms. Leah Mashaka (Nyang'holongo Village Executive Officer) for their cooperation in giving out secondary data and also for their commitment in working with us during interviews and questionnaires of the business owners and communities in Usagara and Nyang'holongo villages.

References:

AAH (2012) Action Against Hunger; *Rural-Urban Linkages in Guinea*, www.actionagainsthunger.org.uk.

Alemu, E.A. and J.Adesina(2017) In Search of Rural Entrepreneurship: Non-farm Household Enterprises (NFEs) as Instruments of Rural Transformation in Ethiopia: In Search of Rural Entrepreneurship, African Development Review 29(2):259-271.

Amankwah-Amoah, J. (2017). Cultivating greater self-confidence in African management research. *Thunderbird International Business Review* 60:511-522

Anríquez, G. (2007) Long-term rural demographic trends. FAO, Rome

Anríquez, G and L. Stloukal (2008) Rural Population Change in Developing Countries: Lessons for Policymaking. European View, vol. 7, 2: pp. 309-317.

Bah, M., Cisse, S., Diyamett, B., Diallo, G., Lerise, F., Okali, D., Okpara, E., Olawoye, J., and C. Tacoli (2003) Changing rural-urban linkages in Mali, Nigeria and Tanzania, *Environmental and Urbanization*.

Baumgartner, D., Schulz, T., and Seidl, I. (2013). Quantifying entrepreneurship and its impact on local economic performance: A spatial assessment in rural Switzerland and *Entrepreneurship & Regional Development*, 25(3-4), 222-250.

Berger, A. N and G.F. Udell (2006) A more complete conceptual framework for SME finance. *Journal of Banking and Finance, 30*(11), 2945–2966.

Bergman, M. M. (2009b) "The Straw Men of the Qualitative-Quantitative Divide and their Influence on Mixed Methods"; *Advances in Mixed-methods Research*, Sage Thousands Oaks. Vol. 15, No. 1.

Bird, K., A. Mckay and I. Shinyekwa (2010) Isolation And Poverty: *The relationship between spatially differentiated access to goods and services and poverty*. ODI Working Paper 322, CPRC Working Paper 162(https://www.odi.org/sites/odi.org.uk/files/odi-assets/publications-opinion-files/5516.pdf.

Boianovsky, M (2017) When the history of ideas meets theory: *Arthur Lewis and the classical economists on development*. CHOPE Working Paper, No. 2017-08, Duke University, Center for the History of Political Economy (CHOPE), Durham, NC(http://hdl.handle.net/10419/172300).

Bosore, J and M. Etyang (2003) The effects of Education on Business skills cognition: the case of indigenous microscale enterprise owners in Kenya. Journal of Vocational and Training Vol 55. Number 1(*https://www.tandfonline.com/doi/pdf/10.1080/13636820300200215*).

Burholt, V and D. Naylor (2005) The relationship between rural community type and attachment to place for older people living in North Wales, UK. *European journal of ageing*, 2(2), 109–119.doi:10.1007/s10433-005-0028-3.

Davis, B., Di Giuseppe, S., & Zezza, A. (2017). Are African households (not) leaving agriculture? Patterns of households' income sources in rural Sub-Saharan Africa.*Food policy*, 67, 153–174. DOI:10.1016/j.foodpol.2016.09.018.

Chongela, J (2015) Contribution of the agriculture sector to the Tanzanian economy. American Journal of Research Communication, 3(7):57-70. www.usa-journals.com. ISSN: 2325-4076.

Chow, I. H (2006) The relationship between entrepreneurial orientation and firm performance in China. SAM Advanced Management Journal, 71(3), 11-21.

Cresswell, J.W and V.L. Plano (2011). Designing and conducting mixed-method research. 2nd Sage; Thousand Oaks, CA: [Google Scholar].

Enders, A., & Jelassi, T. (2000). The converging business models of the Internet and bricks-and-mortar retailers. European Management Journal, 18(5), 542-550.

Ferris, S., R.Peter, B. Rupert, D. Seville, A. Buxton, J. Shriver and E. Wei (2014) Linking smallholder farmers to markets and the implications for extension and advisory services.

MEAS discussion paper 4 (*https://www.agrilinks.org/.../MEAS% 20 Discussion%20Paper%204%20-%20Linking%...*)

Gallaugher, J. M. (2002). 'E-commerce and the undulating Distribution Channels.' Communications of the ACM, 45, 7(2002), 89-95.

Grewal, B., H. Grunfred and P Sheehan (2012)The contribution of agricultural growth to poverty reduction.ACIAR Impact Assessment Series Report No. 76. Australian Centre for International Agricultural Research: Canberra. 59 pp.

IFPRI (2000) Agriculture in Tanzania Since 1986: Follower or Leader of Growth? *A World Bank Country Study*. June 2000. World Bank. Washington

Isinika, A. C., Ashimogo, G. C. and Milangwa, J. E. D. 2005. From Ujamaa to structural adjustment- Agricultural intensification in Tanzania. *In:* Djurfeldt, G., Holmén, H., Jirstrõm, M. and Larsson, R. (eds.) *The African food crisis: lessons from the Asian green revolution.* Wallingford: CABI International.

Javis, D. and P. Dunham (2003) "Conceptualising the 'competitive' strategies of rural manufacturing SMEs", in TijdschriftvoorEconomische en Sociale Geografic, volume 94, no. 2, pp. 246-257.

Kay, C (2009) Development strategies and rural development: exploring synergies, eradicating poverty, The Journal of Peasant Studies, 36:1, 103-137, DOI:10.1080/03066150902820339.

Kinda, T and J.Loening (2010) Small Enterprise Growth and the Rural Investment Climate: Evidence from Tanzania. Munich Personal RePEc Archive, Paper No. 25894, (https://mpra.ub.uni-muenchen.de/25894/).

Kothari C.R. (2004). Research methodology: Methods & Techniques. New Age International (P) Ltd, Publishers.New Delhi India.

Lanjouw, J. O. and Lanjouw, P. (2001). The Rural Non-Farm Sector: Issues and Evidence from Developing Countries. Agricultural Economics, 26:1-23.

Lele, U and J.W. Mellor (1981). "Technological Change, Distributive Bias and Labor Transfer in a Two-Sector Economy," Oxford Economic Papers, Oxford University Press, vol. 33(3), pages 426-441.

Lewis, W.A. (1954) Economic Development with Unlimited Supplies of Labour. The Manchester School of Economic and Social, 22, 139-191

Loscocco, K. A. and Leicht, K. T. (1993) "Gender, work-family linkages, and economic success among small business owners", in Journal of Marriage and the Family, volume55, pp. 875-887.

Maxwell, S., I, Urey and C. Ashley (2001) Emerging issues in rural development, an issue paper - odi.org (*https:// www.odi.org/resources/docs/5898*.pdf).

McKenzie, David and Christopher Woodruff (2014) "What are we learning from business training evaluations around the developing world?",*World Bank Research Observer*, 29(1): 48-82.

Muravyev, A., Talavera, O and D. Schäfer (2009) Entrepreneurs' gender and financial constraints: evidence from international data. *Journal of Comparative Economics, 37*(2), 270–286. https:// doi.org/10.1016/j.jce.2008.12.001.

Naude, W. (2011). Entrepreneurship is not a Binding Constraint on Growth and Development in the Poorest Countries. World Development, 39 (1):33-44.

Osterwalder, A. and Y. Pigneur(2010) *Business Model Generation: A Handbook for Visionaries, Game Changers, and Challengers*, Wiley, Hoboken.

Page, J (2016) Industry in Tanzania: Performance, prospects, and public policy (https://www.wider.unu.edu/sites/default/files/wp2016-5.pdf).

Pathak, S., Goltz, S and M. Buche (2013). Influences of gendered institutions on women's entry in entrepreneurship", International Journal of Entrepreneurial Behaviour and Research, 19(5), in press

Pingali P. L. (2012). Green revolution: impacts, limits, and the path ahead. *Proceedings of the National Academy of Sciences of the United States of America*, *109*(31), 12302-8.

Ranis, G. (2004). Arthur Lewis's Contribution To Development Thinking and policy.*Manchester School*, 72(6), pp.712-723.

Ravallion, M., S. Chen, and P. Sangraula (2007)."New Evidence on the Urbanization of Global Poverty."Background note for the World Development Report 2008, The World Bank, Washington, D.C.

Smitka, M (1998) The Japanese economic history 1600-1960, Washington and Lee University, New York.

Statistics Canada (1999a) 1996 Census Dictionary (Ottawa: Statistics Canada, Catalogue no.92-351).

Steiner, A., & Markantoni, M. (2013).Exploring community resilience in Scotland through the capacity for change. *Community Development Journal 48(3)*, 1-19.

Steiner, A., & Atterton, J. (2014).The contribution of rural businesses to community resilience.*Local Economy 29 (3)*, 219-235.

Steinfield, C., Adelaar, T., & Lai, Y. J. (2002).Integrating brick and mortar locations with e-commerce: Understanding synergy opportunities. In System Sciences, 2002.HICSS. Proceedings of the 35th Annual Hawaii International Conference on (pp. 2920-2929). IEEE.

Tanzania Census (2012) Population and Housing Census: Basic Demographic and Socio- Economic Profile, Daressalaam. Tanzania.

Therkildsen, O (2011) Policymaking and implementation in agriculture: Tanzania's push for irrigated rice, DIIS working paper 2011, ISBN: 978-87-7605-475-5(*https:// www.files.ethz.ch/isn/134386/DIIS % 20wp % 202011-26% 20til%20web.pdf*).

Timmer, P. C (1988) The agricultural transformation; In Handbook of development economics, Chapter 8: 275-331(https://www.sciencedirect.com/science/ article/pii/S1573447188010113).

Urban, B. (2004).Understanding the moderating effect of culture and self-efficacy on entrepreneurial intentions. Doctoral thesis submitted at the University of Pretoria in April 2004.

UN (2018) United Nations, Department of Economic and Social Affairs, Population Division (2017). *World Population Prospects: The 2017 Revision, Key Findings and Advance Tables*. Working Paper No.ESA/P/ WP/248.

URT (2016) Agricultural sector development programme phase two (ASDP II) (*www.tzdpg.or.tz/.../ ASDP2_Final_Document_20_May._2016__after_edit_ _1_.pdf*)

URT (2013) *The 2012 Population and Housing Census; Population Distribution by Age and Sex*: National Bureau of Statistics, Ministry of Finance, Dar es Salaam; and Office of the Chief Government Statistician, Ministry of State, President's Office, State House, and Good Governance Zanzibar.

Wiklund, J and D. Shepherd (2003) Knowledge-based resources, entrepreneurial orientation, and the performance of small and medium-sized businesses. Strategic Management Journal, 24, 1307-1314.

World Bank (2007a), *Tanzania Pilot Rural Investment Climate Assessment: Stimulating Non-farm Microenterprise Growth*, Report No. 40108-TZ, Washington DC.

Zaridis, A.D and D.T. Mousiolis (2014)Entrepreneurship and SME's Organizational Structure. Elements of a Successful Business, Procedia - Social and Behavioral Sciences 148:463.

THE RISE OF NIGHT MARKETS IN URBAN AREAS: TRANSFORMING COMMUNITY BUSINESSES THROUGH WOMEN AND YOUTH EMPOWERMENT

DELPHINE KESSY[1] AND CONSTANTINE BUSUNGU[1]

1. Department of Tourism and Hospitality Management
St. Augustine University of Tanzania

Introduction and Background

Public spaces attract different activities that support public life, especially in urban areas. The spaces are designed for different activities: including night markets. In Tanzania, the designing of public places specifically, for markets in the past was a result of the community's search for a place to conduct business to support their daily lives. In most cases, the markets were in open-air and/or in the streets which allowed a wide range of socio-economic activities to take place. In recent time, planning and designing science has resulted in setting not only market places but also other facilities such as recreational parks and the conversion bazaars. Night markets are important events in city life because they offer many benefits to the people residing around such areas, most importantly, economic and social benefits rather than buzzing.

According to the literature reviewed by the researchers, night markets play an important role not only in city life but also in attracting tourists. The case of Taiwan's night markets by (Valks, 2014) demonstrated how night markets are busiest places where many things take place at the same time. They include activities such as vendors who are selling food, clothing, and appliances of the sort which are considered inexpensive. Night markets are "markets that offer a wide variety of authentic food and drink as well as unique products and in general, they are extremely crowded areas usually located in narrow alleys/black streets making them extremely busy during peak hours until closing, which is usually around midnight.". While analyzing Factors Influencing the Performance of Night Market Traders in Malaysia, Salleh, *et al,* (2012) found that the most significant factors persuading the night markets are product demands, business life span, the number of employees, the amount of start-up capital and the frequency of weekly trading. Also, it includes the technical resources that are critical to the success and long life of rural micro-businesses.

Peculiar to all the factors is the importance of gender that has been identified as one of the success factors that contribute to the long life of many businesses. Despite those facts, urbanization and industrialization have been categorized among the push factors that force youth and women to leave their rural homes to urban areas where they expect to be employed. The rural areas where agricultural activities are practiced were thought to contribute less to the earning potentials of the rural dwellers as earlier proclaimed by Lewis, 1954. Hence, the non-farm enterprises became important both to urban and rural development and their contribution has never been reported to decline (Nagler & Naud´e, 2014).

This study aimed at studying two cases of night markets in the City of Mwanza to examine their growth, characteristics, and impacts on the urban community businesses transformation as a result of youth and women empowerment. The significance of this study comes under the assumption that the changes in traditional retail and commercial activities were the major influence of public places which created a sense of buzzing environment in a traditional way of living. However, that realm of public space is being replaced by modern shopping centers and malls such as the Rock City Mall in Mwanza with few opportunities offered for local businesses. The Unemployment rate is estimated to be at 22.3 percent against 7.1 percent in urban and rural areas respectively in Tanzania. The modern business areas are argued to drive out the local businesses and provide no unique culture, product, appearance or identity and even more they lead to loss of identity and uniqueness of the shopping environment as significant types of public spaces in the cities. Women and youth between 15 and 35 years old are major victims of insecurity, unemployment and consequently poverty therefore they are thought to set a time bomb in Tanzania's economic development. The modern shopping centers are potentially a source of both employment, particularly among women and youth but not as it might be compared with the rise of night markets.

Thus, this study answered the following research problems: what are the components and attributes of the night markets in Mwanza? what are the impact of women and youth empowerment to the night markets? what are the buyers' expectations and evaluation of the services of the night markets? what are the impacts of the night businesses to the communities in Mwanza? Both theoretical, empirical and actual studies were conducted to understand the impact of the rise of night markets in the city of Mwanza. The research was grounded on the pull and push factors theory that was blended to the empowerment. The perception of the urban designing and psychological ties of people to the environment was also of great concern for this study. The actual study was limited to the impact of the rise of night markets in the city of Mwanza in the context of Igoma and Buhongwa markets. The significant characteristics of these markets which resulted in their high impact in the city were results of site visits and different interviews conducted to youth and women in the two markets. Therefore, the perceptual findings are limited to the time the study was conducted but has a comparative value for other markets in and outside Mwanza.

Literature Review

Theories and Framework: *Push and Pull Factor Theory*

While examining the pull and push elements of entrepreneurship in small-scale mining, Mkubukeli, Z & Cronje, JC (2018) observed that:

> "The Push and Pull Factor theory of entrepreneurship takes the view that there are two main reasons that make people decide to become entrepreneurs. The theory suggests that some people are forced into entrepreneurship by their circumstances, while others are enticed or drawn into entrepreneurship because of their expertise and skills or an opportunity that presents itself".

Muthuraman and Haziazi (2018) assert that individuals are pushed into entrepreneurship by negative external factors like job dissatisfaction, dismissal from a job and many other adverse circumstances such as high levels of unemployment and poverty are among them. Unemployed women and youths are more likely to engage in anti-social activities and descend into crime (Fatoki, 2014; Turton and Herrington, 2012). Muthuraman and Haziazi (2018) found that when the economy is slow and the unemployment rate is high, people are forced to start their own businesses to make a living. However, businesses that ran out of necessity have little impact on economic growth although a family's inadequate economic situation can influence a woman to choose entrepreneurship to earn an income. The Pull theory suggests that individuals are attracted to entrepreneurial activities in order to seek independence, to use their skills and experience in an optimal way (Muthuraman and Haziazi, 2018). Mitchelmore and Rowley (2013) report that in 2010, 104 million women in 59 economies representing more than 52 percent of the world's population and 84 percent of world GDP embarked on new venture creation and development. Return on investment for women is much higher than that of men. Women seem to have more responsibilities in the family than men so engaging themselves in business is an opportunity to earn more income for their family.

On the other hand, a high percentage of youth may lack the necessary skills and the necessary network to acquire information on job opportunities. Chigunta (2002) stated that youth and women apply the enterprising qualities, such as initiative, innovation, creativity, and risk-taking into the work environment (either in self-employment or employment in small start-up firms), using the appropriate skills necessary for success in that environment and culture. Despite that fact, a business place where clients or buyers a found and night markets are one of such places. The markets are open spaces either set apart for that particular purpose or they develop as a result of an opportunity seen out of them. Although without skills and knowledge youth and women operating their businesses in the open-air markets take some risk. They become aware of business ownership as a viable alternative, develop an idea for the business while at the same time they learn the process of becoming an entrepreneur and undertake the initiation and development of a business (Fatoki, 2014). Women and youth skills at this juncture rely much on their traditional activities, "agriculture and cooking for women". Hence most of them find themselves in selling fresh vegetables, fruits and many others of the sort. The food vending business is the key of all especially because all the businessmen and women in the markets have to eat. To summarize, the following are the pull and push factors for youth and women entrepreneurship that may contribute to the growth of night markets:

Serial Number	PUSH FACTORS (necessity-based)	PULL FACTORS (opportunity-based)
1	Unemployment	Independence
2	Lack of job	Autonomy
3	Unacceptable job conditions	Risk-taking
4	Professional frustration (Lack of the necessary skills)	Self-achievement
5	Lack of network to acquire information on job opportunities.	Innovation
6	Economic necessity (women have responsibilities in the family)	Job satisfaction
7	Job dismissal	Creativity
8	Looking for basic needs	Desire for wealth

Table 7.1: The Push and Pull Factors for Women and Youth Entrepreneurship
Source: Adapted from Muthuraman and Haziazi, 2018

Lewis Model of Economic Development

In 1954, W. A. Lewis introduced the theory of economic development. In this model, he postulated that there is an unlimited supply of labor that could be available at subsistence wages and that with time, production would grow with an accumulation of capital. The unlimited supply of labor occurred in places where the population was so large relative to capital, for example in Tanzania. In such places, the capital is scarce and is not spread finely to all over the labor - not to mention the unemployed population. In such places or countries, industries are undeveloped and so they are a few compared to the demand for employment. Thus, income growth and distribution are also low (Muthuraman and Haziazi, 2018). Such a condition force people to seek capital to allow themselves to engage in small businesses that can earn them some income although such an earning may not contribute much to economic development. Lewis argued that the use of the capitalist surplus enables the expansion of the economy. The surplus is, however, the profit that is made out of investment and it should be reinvested to create new capital and employment out of subsistence sectors.

Apart from agriculture, another large subsistence sectors are the range of casual jobs, for example, workers on the docks, the porter, the jobbing gardener, and the petty retail trading (Lewis, 1954). Hence, even by running away from agricultural activities the petty business traders in the markets are subsistence traders because their capital is small and they sell agricultural related products that are crowded with stalls of different types and the earning is only for supporting their living. Chongela (2015) observed that more than 67 percent of Tanzanians live in rural areas where most of the natural resources are found. Apart from being important for tourism development, natural resources are important as a major source of raw materials for industry development.

In the end, Lewis (1954) maintained that the capitalist might be stopped when the price of subsistence goods rises or the price is not falling as fast as subsistence productivity per head is raising or because capitalists' workers raise their subsistence standards. Tanzania is not a capitalist country, thus, the buyer's expectations of the markets are such as small agri-processing industries (due to increase in knowledge and skills for doing the businesses) which are re-investing their profit for their expansion and to create more employment opportunities, less generic of imported products, cheaper price but of quality products that satisfy their needs (Chigunta, 2002 & Fatoki, 2014).

Conceptualizing the Rise of Open- Air Markets

The urban design is a result of the emphasis that is placed on people when they perceive, value and draw and add meaning to the urban environment. On the one hand, people migrate to urban areas in most cases to look for a job. They move from rural areas especially during food shortages and unemployment. Lewis (1954) pointed out that food shortage problems could be overcome by importing in an open economy. In rural areas, women are breadwinners for most African families. Both women and youth are involved in different agriculture activities but women suffer the most because during the harvest season they never get enough compensation as compared to the energy put in.

Meanwhile, men are the main beneficiaries of the harvest. Therefore, the youth escapes the rural setting to look for some source(s) of incomes in urban areas. Another important reason as why the youth and women look for alternative activities to agriculture is the owner's operation structure of agriculture and the urban informal sector which lacks capital and little wages respectively. As a result, women and youth are forced to look for employment in order to cater to life's high needs such as food, shelter and marry among others. They are forced to migrate to urban areas only to involve themselves in different activities such as selling farm produces, food vending and many other informal businesses. Their ideal place for conducting businesses is in an open-air market where in most cases at the start there exist little or no legal bindings. On the other hand, in urban areas, life demands are many and difficult to attain. Hence, women and youth of the urban areas who represent a high unemployment rate have to look for employment. Therefore, engage themselves in small business activities.

The act of doing business in open-air places is a result of environmental perception. People and the environment affect each other. The perception placed on the environment is a result of stimuli such as sight, sound, smell or tactile information which are the evidence surrounding us. Perception is the act of making sense of pieces shreds of evidence found in the environment. In doing so, people reduce reality to a selective impression of place images. It is argued that one of the major characteristics of the place is its power to order and to focus on human intentions, experience, and behavior spatially, therefore, the place is an interaction of physical setting, activity, and meaning (Sime, 1986; Relph, 1976). Migrants from rural areas make meaning of the urban areas in which during the struggle to meet life demands in urban life they utilize the open spaces in the streets resulting in the development of open-air markets and designing of the same. The open-air markets are seen as important dimensions of Mwanza city development.

Attributes of the Night Markets

There are many different existing night markets in the world such Forodhani garden in Zanzibar, Kampala night market in Uganda, Ningxia night market in Taipei and Richmond night market in Canada to mention but a few. Malaysian night market is one of the most famous night markets and it is based on the concept of open-air shopping and the street hawkers or petty traders occupy a designated part of the street to set up their stalls. Lee *et al*, (2016) identified several characteristics of the night markets which are based on their nature of the operation. They assert that night markets take place in the night mainly in the urban or suburban areas that are thought to have more leisurely strolling, shopping and eating areas than more businesslike day markets. The markets have unique consumption activities, displays, products, and bargain prices which reflect the history, society, and economics. In Malaysia, the night markets reflect the Malaysian culture. In other places, the night markets offer entertainment, sell traditional products such as casual clothes, fruits, exotic, snacks and novelty items.

According to Yu (2004), night markets are hot and noisy such that some people would not want to be neighbors to them. People rather prefer their neighborhoods to be quiet and orderly rather than chaotic, and noisy. Despite that fact, night markets offer services to the after-work group of people who do not have a good day time shopping. The physical location is convenience especially because public transport is always available and the best to use during the night. The night markets, the small businesses offer a variety of cheap products.

Contribution of women and youth to the night markets

The Association of International Research and Development Centers for Agriculture (AIRCA) acknowledges that women and youth constitute "a large proportion of the agricultural labor force (43 percent and of farmers in developing countries" and above 60 percent for youth in East Africa's Lake Victoria Basin. Because the average productivity for women is lower by 20-30 percent of the men, many efforts and emphasis have been placed on women so to increase their productivity. Working with women increases the chances of increasing household income and decrease poverty in their families. Women engage in entrepreneurship programs out of necessity rather than an opportunity (Muthuraman and Haziazi, 2018). Youth do not see agriculture as an opportunity in their rural setting because they lack the necessary skills and many other important resources such as capital for its development. AIRCA adds that smallholder farmers lack access to credit and markets for the products.

As a result, there have been many empowerment programs both to women and youth; some of them focusing on agriculture development related issues, for example, training in vegetables growing from cultivation techniques to production, finances, and marketing (AIRCA). Skills acquired from such programs enable trainees to search for possible ways to increase their earning potential. One of them is to embark on small and medium enterprises development. However, the later does not work well in the rural setting. Hence, everyone hypothesized that urban areas are a good source of income resulting in rural-urban migration. In urban areas, women and youth are involved in different activities such as selling vegetable produce, food vending, selling of cloth and many other sort items. Because of the financial constraints, their capital is always small which forces them to form small but important groups that enable them to secure some funds. These groups which are more or less like Savings and Credit Co-operative Society (SACCOS) are informal but they serve more than one purpose; that securing funds and security at the same time.

The Case Studies

Buhongwa and Igoma Night Markets

Buhongwa and Igoma markets are just two of very few markets around Mwanza where one can get a wide variety of food sold at comparatively cheap prices (Stephen, 2012). Buhongwa market was established in 2008 as a farmer's market. Before that time people used to shop at Mkuyuni and at the main market at the heart of the city of Mwanza. Buhongwa market was not established as a night market but due to the increasing demand for its services it operates till night. The market, therefore, officially operates from 6 am to 11 pm although one can work for 24 hours. The police do conduct patrols to ensure the security of the areas.

Unlike Igoma, Buhongwa is a designed market although not along the road reserves. The market is having around 508 petty businesses during the day but the number is higher in the morning due to temporary vendors who bring in the fresh farm produce. The market sells vegetables, fruits, fish, clothes, utensils and electrical appliances to mention but a few. Buhongwa market is located in Buhongwa, one of the Mwanza City wards with a population of 26,681 according to the 2012 census and a population change of 121.7% compared to the 2002 census. The market is specifically found along Mwanza – Shinyanga road about 9 kilometers from the Mwanza city center where transport is guaranteed for both buyers and sellers. Buhongwa forms 17.6 percent of the Mwanza city area whereas the total area of the city is 25,233.0 square kilometers of the whole Mwanza region. Mwanza region has a total area of 256 square kilometers.

Igoma market started between 2005 – 2008 with two individuals. The market sits along the Mwanza - Musoma road reserve in Igoma ward, a few kilometers after Nyakato national. Along the Mwanza – Musoma road about 10 kilometers from the city center. Before the commencement of this market people used to buy from the "soko la chini" place. Much of the farm produce is from farmers themselves. Traders work until 10 pm but in the past, there was no limit especially for food vendors and motorcycles. The market has about 2500 vendors but the active members could be 500. There is a space planned for the market but apparently it is faced by two major problems; one, it is small in the midst of human settlement and two, it is a small area of about 2 acres that cannot carry 2500 registered petty traders. Because the market is not at its planned place, the petty traders are sometimes asked to leave which results in problems such as failing to make loan repayments in case one is having a bank loan and loss of customers resulting in frustration. The market is clean and because it is located along the road, transport is guaranteed when shopping there. Igoma covers 16.0 percent of all the city area and its population is 56,596 with a population change of 56.5% (National Bureau of Statistics, 2016).

> "The 2011 Economic Survey Report shows that Mwanza region's share of the national GDP for the year 2016 was only 9.3 percent equivalent to Tanzania Shillings 8,452,013 million while per capita income of regional residents were estimated to be Tshs. 2,004,353, (equivalent to US$ 911.1 at a rate of TZS 2,200 per USD)". (Mwanza City Council Socio-Economic Profile 2016).

The profile recognizes the selling of raw food or uncooked food as one of its main sources of income. Its contribution comes from 13.6 percent of the total residence in it right after commercial food crops and forestry which is by engaged 13.9 percent of the residence. Other sources of income are trade and commerce (12.9 percent of population), manufacturing (11.7 percent), construction (7.2 percent), services for food hotel and lodges (5.5 percent), domestic services (5.0 percent), haulage and storages (4.7 percent), administration and security services (3.3 percent), education services (3.1 percent) and fishing, hunting, livestock and other related (2.5 percent). Buhongwa and Igoma markets approximately serve around 400,000 and 600,000 people while accommodating an average of 500 trade vendors involved in selling and buying of the agricultural produces. In a day, a trader may serve about 30 buyers. Some of the produces found in the markets are maize, groundnuts, cassava, sweet potatoes, bananas, Irish potatoes, onions, fruits, millet, sorghum, vegetables and electrical appliances of the sort to mention but a few. All farm produce areas sold while fresh and most of them look organic. The markets serve as one-point for all household required items. Clothes are also available in these markets. People from different areas travel so they may shop from these markets.

To ensure smooth functioning, the markets established a set of rules which govern them. The current rules are:

- An applicant for any business activity is required to pay application fees which are around Tanzania shillings 100,000 to get a business space

- Every trader is required to contribute some money for keeping the working environment clean either daily or monthly and that payment covers all the working hours of the market. However, every trader in the market must keep his/her space clean.

- The selling of animals like goats, sheep, and hens is by permission, especially from the administration.

- Unloading from vehicles must be between one and two hours after the arrival. No vehicle movements around the shed grounds where vendors are selling their items especially when the market is open

- All vendors must respect themselves, yet illegal businesses such as drugs are not allowed.

- Customers and or vendor's complaints that cannot be resolved amicably should be referred to the market administration.

Methods

The research employed a qualitative approach in a case study strategy. Normally case studies are useful for learning about a little or inadequately known situations so to make them know (Pacho, 2015). The outcome may be called lessons learned from a real-life setting and could be applied or adapted to other settings of similar problems. Qualitative studies are rich in description of phenomena which allows the researcher to such a problem from participants' point of view (Cresswell, 2012). If two cases are studied, the researcher should describe one case at a time hence the survey of the cases of this research followed that procedure. Qualitative studies do not make heavy use of measurement or statistics (Denzin & Lincoln, 2000) but they are descriptive and exploratory; and sensitive to the social construction of meaning (empirical and inductive in nature) and rely on interpretation and analysis of what people do and say. The information collected is about perceptions, beliefs, opinions, emotions, and existing relationships of individuals and the natural world. This study was informed by thirty (30) respondents. Their specific predictions, the narration of facts and their characteristics are transcribed in the following section. Despite that qualitative studies make little use of statistical data which hinders their extrapolation to other places but useful for comparative studies (Cresswell, 2012). The flowing figure represents a summary of how the research was carried out.

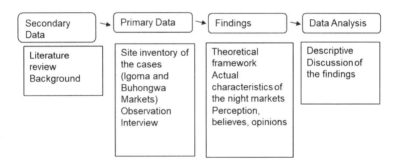

Figure 7.1. Pictorial Presentation of the Research Strategy

Findings and Discussion

Attributes of the Buhongwa and Igoma Night markets

The composition of the markets, the people and the way the markets are arranged from the first part of their attributes. Thus, the aim of this objective was to study how such attributes contribute to the rise of the markets. They are presented as follows:

Respondents Characteristics

The study focused on youth thus, the most significant characteristics of the respondents were age and gender. Both genders played major roles in different business activities except that females were not seen in barbershops. Youth, both male and female (age 18-40), represented 64 percent of all the respondents while older (age 41 and above) were 36 percent. Youth especially, the male could do all types of businesses including the loading and unloading of goods or load which their counterpart could not do. However, females were seen to assist buyers with their small goods from a specified place to the other. Female (both youth and older) represented 67 percent of all the respondents while the male was 33 percent. For the female, 60 % were youth while their male counterpart was 70%. The age and gender distribution of the respondent are presented in table 7.2 below followed by their corresponding pie charts.

Gender	Category of Gender	Age	Sample Size	Total Male/Female	% Youth/Older	% Total
Male	Youth	18 -40	7	10	70	33
	Older	41 and above	3		30	
Female	Youth	18-40	12	20	60	67
	Older	41 and above	8		40	
Total			30			100

Table 7.2. Gender and Age Distribution of the Respondents

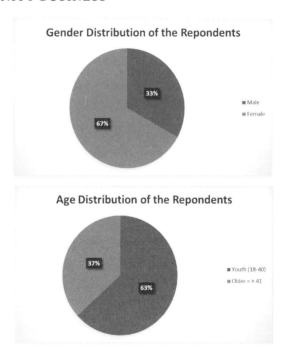

Level of education

Many respondents were educated at the levels of primary and secondary education and business skills (46.7 and 36.7 percent, n = 30 respectively). A percentage of 16.7 represented those who were educated in other types of education but informal. About 90 percent of the respondents have had some training in business skills development and management. The level of education is represented in the pie chart below.

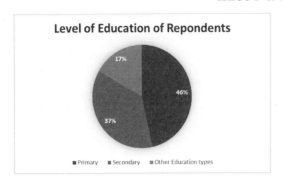

Figure 7.2. Level of Education of Respondents

Price of the Products

It was difficult to record the price list of all the products sold in both the markets. However, a few of the items were taken because the price was among the significant factors that contributed to consumer choices of the markets. Despite that, all the merchandises in the markets were generally considered to be charged low or reasonable prices as compared to other markets except for imported products such as electric appliances, clothes, and machines. The prices were cheaper compared to the prices of the same products sold in super or mini – supermarkets or even the shopping malls, such as the Rock City Mall. For example, a kilogram of meat was sold at 5,000 in Buhongwa while in the supermarkets it was at 8,000. However, there is no consistency in prices. At times a kilogram of meat raises to 6,000 and a year or so ago a kilogram was sold at 6,500. The same applies to fish. This time around the Nile perch fish of about 2 kilograms was sold at between 9,000 and 12,000 instead of between

12,000-16,000. Tilapia price, however, remained constant or there was no significant difference between eight months before this study was conducted and when it was conducted. For almost two years until when this study was conducted the price of a kilogram of meat remained constant. Prices for other subsistent goods such as vegetables, maize, beans, yams, potatoes and the like were changing although at smaller margins.

Other characteristics

It was clearly stated that Buhongwa and Igoma markets operate both day and night starting from 6 am to 11 pm and 6 am to 10 pm at night respectively. The markets have common characteristics as described below:

- **Accessibility.** Both Buhongwa and Igoma markets are located along the main roads. People from different places may access them easily. The accessibility gives the market an advantage for operating until 11 pm.

- **They are farmers' markets.** Both markets are referred to as farmers' markets. They sell fresh farm produce apart from other items. However, although fresh, most of the food and fruits were in raw form which would require the buyer to take a long time in preparation. There were a few agri-processing industries such as milling machines and groundnuts grinders.

Respondent A at Igoma market said,

"my suppliers may supply about 5 tonnes of sweet potatoes in a week. The potatoes come from different parts of Mwanza such as Sengerema, Katubilo, Nyanguge, and even Geita. I, myself sell to between 35 and 45 customers in a day. Without this market, I do not know where would I be now".

Respondent D in Buhongwa said,

"As you see, I am a vegetable vendor. I come to this market to buy vegetables and tomatoes. They are always fresh and sold at the cheapest price compared to other markets. See this pineapple, it only sold at Tanzanian shillings 2,000".

- **Night hours of operation.** Buhongwa and Igoma markets operate from morning hours 10 and 11 pm in the night respectively. The pick hours are 19 to 21 hours. At this time the markets are crowded.

- **A mixture of products.** Apart from the farm products, modern items such as generic of imported products like clothes, shoes, soaps, telephone accessories, equipment and electric appliances from China and the neighboring countries of Kenya and Uganda were identified. Others are machines such as sewing machines, grinding machines, and apples that were imported from South Africa. A few of the cultural and local made shoes and clothes were found.

- **Safety.** At markets, it was known that money is constantly changing hands and therefore raises the question of safety. Buhongwa and Igoma displayed concrete efforts to keep the markets through a well-established safety system under the market administration. However, a few cases of cheating might occur.

    Respondent B asserted that,

    > "Cheating appears mostly between a seller and buyer and sometimes between seller and seller especially when there is an act of trust in assisting each other and which is not supported by legal binding".

- **Readily available food.** It is common in Buhongwa and Igoma markets to find food vendors selling food that is ready to eat. In their small stall, women arrange about three or four "desks" and small tables good enough for customers to eat from. The food stall serves men and women working in the markets and most importantly, the youth who are not yet married.

    Respondent C respondent that,

    > "I eat here every day after my daily activities. You know what! as I am not married it is not easy for me to cook at home so what I do is to pass here after the job, take my meal and off I go. On getting home, it is only a matter of going to bed".

- **Noisy.** The markets are noisy, making the surrounding community feel anxious although they help them. When asked if they did not like the market Respondent E said,

> "the market helps us a lot yet it has employed a lot of women and youth. If it is stopped that means denying them many opportunities. Where will they go? We are already used to that noisy, we do not feel disturbed anymore".

Women and youth contribution to the night markets in Mwanza

Women and youth form the highest percentage of respondents (67 and 64, respectively) in Buhongwa and Igoma markets. They are the major traders in the markets. The Pull and Push factor theory was proved to contribute to the growth of the Buhongwa and Igoma markets and so the engagement of women and youth in trading in both markets. Working in the markets was a result of little capital which could not be used to do other business types. Some started with a capital of Tanzania shillings 50,000 and grew to 500,000. The most contributing factor was the trust they had decided to put on each other. That served as a security to get a loan which was obtained in the form of a merry-go-round.

It was revealed that some traders could obtain loan from formal SACCOS, free interest loan governments although in small amounts and other from banks. The traders dealt with what they knew the best. 60 percent of the respondents (n = 30) acknowledged that they get their supplies from farmers and that some of them (51 percent) came from the rural areas through invitation by their relatives to do the petty business. Some of the vegetable vendors are the peasant farmers themselves and some of them use a bicycle to bring their products to the markets. When asked to rank the reasons for doing business in the markets the lack of job, unemployment and economic necessity were the most significant push factors as they ranked number one to three consecutively while from the pull factors the need to be independence/autonomy and the act of taking risk ranked the highest. Table 7.3 below represents the ranking of the pull and push factors for conducting business in both markets. However, not many of the respondents have attended training regarding business operations.

PUSH FACTORS (necessity-based)	Rank	PULL FACTORS (opportunity-based)	Rank
Lack of job	1	Independence/Autonomy	1
Unemployment	2	Risk-taking	2
Economic necessity (women have responsibilities in the family)	3	Creativity	3
Little capital	4	Self-achievement	4
Lack of network to acquire information on job opportunities.	5	Innovation	5
Job dismissal	6	Availability of the social informal institution such as that of merry-go-round; government start-up loan	6

Table 7.3: The ranking of Pull and Push Factors
for Youth and Women Entrepreneurs

Buyers Expectation and Evaluation of the Services of the Night Markets

When asked how they feel to be buying from the markets, buyers seemed to be happy. They find the services perfect for them.

"You see, almost everything here especially food is cheaper compared to other places. I buy fresh vegetables directly from the farmers. What else should we ask? A few more things may be, and this should go to the authorities. To make this market international and attract tourists. I advise even the sellers to change their mindset. They should think international. Let each of them have a stall for selling the items in a more presentable way. That, will convince us, buyers, to keep coming here as we always do and attract even more buyers including the tourists." said Respondent El in Igoma market. "

The Igoma and Buhongwa markets are busiest places. Many customers buy on a weekly basis and daily buyers are those who live nearby the markets themselves. One respondent emphasized that there are no regrets on buying from the Buhongwa market, prices are reasonable and the food is fresh, moreover, the markets are on a daily basis. Except for items like clothes and other non-food items which one may demand some special high-quality brands the markets are perfect for all the buyers, both end -users, and non-end users.

Growth of the Businesses in Igoma and Buhongwa Market

For a shorter period of time, both Igoma and Buhongwa Markets have grown. From the day of their establishment, there has been a rapid increase in the number of petty traders. Igoma market started with only two people but until when this study was conducted the market had registered about 2,500 individuals as petty traders. Of those, it was estimated that 500 were active. In Buhongwa the numbers were far high compared to Igoma. Previously, it was said that the markets started between 2005 – 2008. So depending on the year it started the expansion in four consecutive years could be shown in the following figure.

Figure 7.3. Number of Petty Traders in Igoma

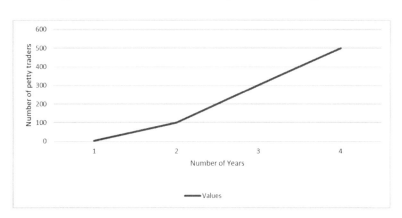

Some of the reasons for the rapid expansion of the petty traders and the expansion of the businesses in the two markets were such as education, an increase in business skills and the lack of employment. The study revealed that 83.4% of the respondents were educated at the level of primary and secondary school and they were as well imparted with some business skills while 16.7% were imparted with both business skills and other informal education such as learning by doing (on the job training). Education played a major role in the success of many small businesses. One respondent stressed "we need those seminars" recalling one business seminar he attended at the St. Augustine University in February 2019.

Another important factor is capital. Some business capital could be as low as 100,000 Tanzanian shillings, which allowed a petty trader to sell assorted fruits. The capital was obtained in the form of donations from organizations such as Lion's club and individual savings. Other reasons were such as conducive business environment, for example, as one-time market duty payment; durability; rapid urbanization of Buhongwa and Igoma - (51 percent of the respondents were from rural areas implying that people were migrating to Igoma and Buhongwa or the nearby places); extent of demand, good transportation and communication, relative low price of the products, security, fresh from farm products and stability of the working places – traders were given specific area such as 2 x 2 meters for working.

The Impacts of the Igoma and Buhongwa Markets on the Communities in Mwanza

1. **Establishment of social services such as police stations** where many people live or stay, security is very important. The police station ensures the

security of the Buhongwa and Igoma areas. Apart from that, sellers have developed their own security system. They even pay watchmen to look after their belongings starting from when they leave for home.

2. **The markets have resulted in the expansion of Mwanza city (Urbanization).** The markets bring services closer to people thus when people see services are available, they feel comfortable about a place, especially for settlement. The markets are known throughout Mwanza and they attract buyers from different places, some from beyond Mwanza city boarders.

3. **Source of government revenue.** The traders do pay market duty

4. **Improved standard of living** – This is a result of earnings that people get every day. Women are able to contribute to their family's well-being. Communities around the markets have also transformed significantly.

5. **Employment** – The markets are a source of employment for more than 500 individuals. Sometimes even the petty traders employ casually especially when the need arises. This is when they need to carry loads of supplies and machine cannot help. Sometimes, people from other small markets can continue to sell in these markets when they run short of customers. Such places are Mkolani and Nyegezi.

6. **Pollution and Congestion** – markets contribute substantially to noise pollution because they bring many people together resulting in congestion. Some environmental and air pollution were noticed as well. Both the markets are congested. Although public parking for public transport is available, there is no enough space for visitors/buyers' private cars parking nor good pathways when shopping around. This prevents many buyers with private vehicles to buy from such markets.

Concluding Remarks

The study found that women engage themselves in trading activities out of necessity and so applies to youth. The pull and push factors for women and youth engagement in entrepreneurial activities that contributed to the growth of Igoma and Buhongwa markets are highlighted in Table 7.3. Buhongwa and Igoma markets although not officially allowed to operate till night, more than 65 percent of youth and women are working there and increase their earning potential for themselves and their families respectively. The operations of the markets looked efficient. It is thought that if they can operate until the late-night the chances are that youth may have more working hours that might contribute substantially in their income. That will guarantee an increase in income for the Mwanza city and the overall Mwanza region. However, security precautions should be taken especially while allowing night market operations.

Also, the study revealed that a few empowerment programs such as training on vegetable production have been conducted to assist women and youth. Many youths conducting businesses in Buhongwa and Igoma markets are from the rural areas although not necessary for Mwanza where there is no employment, capital, and other managerial skills that may help them in agricultural activities. This concurs to Ranis's (2004) findings that owner-operated agriculture and the urban informal sector lack collaborating capital with little wages and so youth and women are forced to look for alternatives in support of their living. The management of free interest government loans and the merry-go-round informal loaning was a result of experience and lessons learned from different places. Also, some respondents explained how the change of mind occurred by getting to know how to serve his customers better especially after they have gotten some business training. It may be concluded that more training is required for both youth and women to enable them to participate in different activities. Also, formal training for loan management might be carried out. Also, it is recommended to strengthen the informal institution such as those of merry -go- round and develop a loan facility specific for youth and women in small businesses not only in the urban areas but also in the rural areas so to foster development.

The study did not find any case about the market prices of commodities such as those of subsistence products that were constant or stable not to decrease nor increase, rather the prices were fluctuating even on a daily basis. Neither did the study found many (even small scaled) agri-processing industries associated with buying farm products in Igoma nor Buhongwa markets. This means Igoma and Buhongwa markets will continue to receive a number of people who will work as petty traders in the markets for some more years because it is cheaper to start and run a business there. The literature revealed that the rural areas still have 67 percent of the population of Tanzania and until when this study was conducted the urban areas had an unemployment rate of 22.3 percent compared to 7.1 percent of the rural areas. Capital has continued to be a scarce resource to foster industrial development. And the high rate of unemployment continues to close the gap of gender-specific jobs to unspecified employment. Everyone is seen to just get and attach to anything given that it contributes to earning. Who will remain in rural areas? What will the youth and women do in town if the rural areas and industries will remain undeveloped? These questions call for immediate action by youth, women, rural and even town development planners design industries that may observe the unemployed as postulated by Lewis.

The study found that there are existing informal ways of accumulating capital for business operations. Such capital enabled the petty traders to open new or expand their businesses. It was informed of a merry-go-round. As a result, it seemed that despite how arguably it could be Buhongwa and Igoma market areas had at their level adopted the Lewis model as described in chapter two. That is to go capitalist. The petty traders were accumulating the surplus from their subsistence activities and reinvest. It is assumed that practice will continue until the surplus labor will finish and that is when the area would be termed as developed.

For the markets to attract more buyers and even tourists as it was mentioned by some respondents, restructuring, and redesign of the markets might be inevitable. That entails having clearer pathways to and from buyers. The markets should include recreational facilities such as an open-air music place that reflect the culture of the area to add to the traditional food and way of living of the places. Tourists are attracted to shop away from home if they find a different environment fascinating as observed by Lee, *et al*, (2016). Taiwan's night market case by Valks (2014) describes how the night markets in Taiwan have been serving as recreational places for visitors. A parking space for visitors/buyers' vehicles should be designed so to increase buyers/visitors to the places.

As compared to Forodhani and Malaysian night markets, it may be concluded that the Igoma and Buhongwa markets were not designed to be working till after 10 or 11 pm respectively. However, the increase in product and service demands have contributed to the expansion of the businesses and so the working hours. That is supported by Salleh (2012) who found that customer demand and the availability of capital are some of the factors persuading the rise of the night markets in Malaysia. Also, this study found that the lack of employment, the availability of capital and the low levels of education and rural-urban migration, good transport and communication systems and the extents of demand contributed to the growth of Igoma and Buhongwa markets. Therefore, people living around Igoma and Buhongwa markets are making effective utilization of such places as a result of human intentions, experience, and behavior so to rise income and make living possible as observed by Relph (1976). In case of any change, Igoma markets traders have to be given space enough to accommodate them all. Moreover, such a market should allow easy access by customers to the markets.

Igoma and Buhongwa night markets had several challenges. One is that the Igoma market is sitting on the road reserve. The market official place is some kilometers away and according to the market chairperson they were once moved there but they lost their customers. Moreover, that area is small compared to the number of petty traders and in the midst of human settlement. As a result, it is advised to design a new market place. Two, both Igoma and Buhongwa had no electricity. In Buhongwa a fellow petty business trader supplied power through generator so that fellow traders could do business. The businessmen and women expressed their high demand for electricity. According to them, they are ready to contribute any resources such as money, so that they might be supplied with electricity.

Acknowledgment

We acknowledge the support of ward executive officers of Igoma and Buhongwa (Esther Ngonyani and Adam Salum respectively) as well as both the management of the market teams especially the chairpersons (David Emmanuel and Nixon Saganda Igoma and Buhongwa respectively) and all the respondents for their contributions in completion of this study.

References:

Association of International Research and Development Centers for Agriculture (AIRCA).www.airca.org/ docs/Lake_Victoria_Women_&_Youth_Concept _Note_Final.pdf. Retrieved June 4, 2019.

Chigunta, Francis (2002), Youth Entrepreneurship: Meeting the Key Policy Challenges; www.youthmetro.org/.../ youth_entrepreneurship_meeting_the_key_policy_ challenge... Retrieved June 6, 2019.

Chongela, J (2015) Contribution of the agriculture sector to the Tanzanian economy. American Journal of Research Communication, 3(7):57-70. www.usa-journals.com. ISSN: 2325-4076.

Creswell, J. W. (2012). Educational Research: Planning, Conducting and Evaluating Quantitative and Qualitative Research. 4th ed. Pearson Education, Inc., 501 Boylston Street, Boston, MA 02116.

Denzin, N.K. and Lincoln, Y.S. (2000). (eds.). Handbook of Qualitative Research. London, Sage Publications.

Fatoki, O. (2014). Factors Motivating Young South African Women to Become Entrepreneurs, Mediterranean Journal of Social Sciences, MCSER Publishing, Rome-Italy. 5(16), 184 – 190. ISSN 2039-2117 (online) ISSN 2039-9340 (print). DOI:10.5901/MJSS. 2014.v5n16p184. Retrieved June 3, 2019.

Lee, S-H., Chang, S-C., Hou, J-S., and Lin, C-H. (2016). Night market experience and image of temporary residents and foreign visitors. https://www.researchgate.net/publication/22905362. Retrieved June 6, 2019.

Lewis, W. A. (1954). Economic Development with Unlimited Supplies of Labour. The Manchester School.

Mitchelmore, S., & Rowley, J (2013). Entrepreneurial competencies of women entrepreneurs pursuing business growth. Journal of Small Business and Enterprise Development, 20(1), 125–142

Mkubukeli, Z & Cronje, JC (2018) Pull and Push Elements of Entrepreneurship in South Africa: A Small-Scale Mining Perspective. J Entrepren Organiz Manag 7: 252. Doi: 10.4172/2169-026X.1000252. Retrieved June 6, 2019.

Muthuraman, S. & Al Haziazi, M. (2018). Pull & Push Motives for Women Entrepreneurs in the Sultanate of Oman. ZENITH International Journal of Multidisciplinary Research. ISSN 2231-5780, 8 (7), 79-95.

Mwanza City Council Socio-Economic Profile 2016 http://mwanzacc.go.tz/storage/app/uploads/public/58c/126dda/58c126dda1c1d467146795.pdf. Retrieved June 6, 2019.

National Bureau of Statistics, (2016). Compiled Data from 2002 and 2012 Population Census Reports, Mwanza Region, 2016

Nagler, P. & Naud´e, W. (2014). Patterns and Determinants of Non-Farm Entrepreneurship in Rural Africa: New Empirical Evidence. 9th IZA/World Bank Conference on Employment and Development 25-26 June 2014 - Lima, Peru.

Pacho, T.O. (2015). Exploring Participants' Experiences Using Case Study. International Journal of Humanities and Social Science, 4 (5), 44-53.

Ranis, G. (2004). Labor Surplus Economies: Economic Growth Center Discussion Paper Series no 900. Yale University. http://www.econ.yale.edu/~egcenter / research.htm.

Relph, E. (1976). Place and placelessness. London: Pion

Salleh, F., Yaakub, N., Yunus, K., Ghani, M. A. & Sulong, Wan K. W. (2012). Factors Influencing the Night Market Traders' Performance in Malaysia, International Journal of Business and Management; Vol. 7, No. 14; 2012. Pp 32-39. ISSN 1833-3850   E-ISSN 1833-8119 Canadian Center of Science and Education.

Sime, J. D. (1986). Creating places or designing spaces? Journal of Environmental Psychology, 6, 49-63.

Stephen, D. (2012). Buhongwa is more than just a food wholesale market. Daily News Report.

Su-Hsin Lee, S., Chang, S., Hou, J. & Lin, C. (2008). Night market experience and image of temporary residents and foreign visitors, International Journal of Culture, Tourism and Hospitality Research; 2 (3), 217-233. Emerald Group Publishing Limited

Turton, N, & Herrington, M, (2013). Global Entrepreneurship Monitor South African 2012 Report. (Online). Available: http://www.gemconsortium.org/ docs/2801/gem-south-africa-2012-report. Retrieved June 6, 2019.

Valks, T. (2014). Taiwan's Night Markets: Battlefield of Identity. Masters' Thesis; https:// openaccess.leidenuniv.nl/bitstream/ handle/1887/29516/Thom%20Valks%20-%20Master% 20Thesis%20Final.pdf?sequence=1. Retrieved June 15, 2019.

Yu, Shuenn-Der. "Hot and Noisy: Taiwan's Night Market Culture." In The Minor Arts of Daily Life: Popular Culture in Taiwan, edited by David K. Jordan, Andrew D. Morris and Marc L. Moskowitz, 129-49. Honolulu: University of Hawai'i Press, 2004.

NEW CONCEPT OF COMMUNITY BUSINESS AND NEW METHOD OF REGIONAL DEVELOPMENT

MAKOTO HAGINO[1] & TETSUYA TAKANO[2]

[1]**Kagoshima University & [2]Satsuma-Sendai City Office**

Introduction: Background of the study

The purpose of this chapter is to define the concept of community business in this book. We had a common understanding of what is a community business from the facts discovered during our workshop in Kagoshima last March 2019[11]. From that common understanding, each author was writing about a community business and adding some facts on this book. We need to define the concept of our community business in economics theory.

At first, we denote the background of this study before thinking logically. We analyzed an inland area of Satsuma-sendai city, the northern area in Kagoshima prefecture, from a point of view of the economic geography in 2014[12].

It has been said that there were too large mountainous areas and could not be explained by *the central place theory* in Japan[13] and this theory is applicable only in two prefectures, Akita and Miyazaki, which holds the large plains in each prefecture. On the other hand, Kagoshima prefecture was divided into 96 municipalities before the municipal merger policy from 2003. The area of Kagoshima prefecture is 9,187km^2. The number of municipalities was too much against nearby prefectures which there were 44 municipals in Miyazaki prefecture before the policy. Its area is 7,735km^2.

From these geographic backgrounds, we began an investigation on the inland area of Satsuma-sendai city, where 4 municipalities merged before the municipal merge —Togo town, Hiwaki town, Iriki town, and Kedoin town. These towns were located on the Sendai River basin. These areas have been depopulated as well as other local districts in Japan, because of the outflow of the population from a rural area to an urban area since the period of the high growth rate of the GDP of Japan in the 1960s. Then, only a few personal management shops remain. These shops are limited to supplying consumer goods or services. Its industry type is limited to a barbershop, a beauty shop or a house eatery. Even more, we found out these shops were located considerably with even distribution (see Fig. 1 and Fig.2).

In these areas, we found out the following findings. First, most families in these areas have cars and go shopping in a large shopping center within 30 minutes frequently. The price of a product or service sold at a large shopping center is cheaper than the price of the small shop near their house. They purchase a specific product from a shop nearby and become good customers for the shop. They do not take the economical rational consumption action. It is the first hypothesis that other non-economic factors influence consumer behavior. Second, even if a shop withdraws from these areas, a new entry will appear (see Table. 1)[14]. It is possible to explain by the economic theory of Chamberlin's monopolistic competition[15]. This theory has been recognized that could apply to a small business in an urban area or suburban area. Our field is a depopulated rural area. Second hypothesis is that monopolistic competition was expanded and applicable to these areas. Third, it seems that the shops locate on an even distribution like the central place theory (see Table. 2.). There are few plains and a lot of hills in this area, which could not form hexagonal market zones in the central place theory. Third hypothesis is that the theory overcome spatial obstacles.

We need to give more rationales for above 3 hypotheses than to get more facts.

Results

At first, we should verify the first hypothesis and consider the reason of non-economical consumer conduct. Residents often go to shopping to a large-scale shopping center, but purchase the specific products and services to a small-scale shop nearby in spite of the higher prices than a shopping center. The residents choose purchasing intentionally. It seems *the differentiation of the store*, which a consumer would select in order to shorten time for purchasing, and prefer a store nearby. However, the residents change purchasing nearby, where they have chances to purchase a cheaper goods and services at large-scale shopping center. This purchasing conduct could not be explained by distance or time.

Changing a viewpoint to the resident's eyes, the self-employed proprietor of the shop nearby is recognized as same as people returning to hometowns or moving to a rural area. The self-employed proprietor is welcomed by the residents in a depopulated area, because his family would increase the sustainability of the local community. The proprietor as the residents play a role not only to supply daily necessities but also to prevent disaster or to conserve their environment. In other words, the community need to invite proprietor's family intentionally in order to push the proprietor social duties. He could not keep business without the clients from residents in the community and should transfer to another area if he refuses social duties. These social duties are not a CSR (Corporate Social Responsibility)[16]. The proprietor could run his shop after he discharged social duties in the community. Residents compel the proprietor to finish social duties. It is not a responsibility.

Moreover, residents have selected a type of industry with some conditions. Primarily, it is necessary for a proprietor to inhabit with his family in the community in order to perform his social duty. The type of industry is selected to a family-owned business under the mom and pop operation. Secondly, the community is troubled with the depopulation and aging. The residents of the community cannot form the fund for business invitations. The type of industry should be lower capital cost and a labor intensive, such as a barbershop, a beauty shop and a house eatery. It is easy for this type to entry from other area and withdrawal from the community, which behavior seems on the basis of a monopolistic competition. Thirdly, there is another condition for these shops that provide daily necessities. Anybody in the community can purchase goods or services from a shop nearby every day and do not have to overdo it. That is a barber shop, a beauty shop or a house eatery.

The second hypothesis is that these areas are able to apply the monopolistic competition. Firms operate their business on their average cost curve along with Chamberlin's definition. From the above results, the residents intend to take non-economic behaviors and to keep a profitable line of business. The entry and exit of shops nearby denote a similar behavior to shops under the monopolistic competition. This profitable line corresponds to their average cost curve. It is not the result of competition but of non-economic consumer behavior. Then, the residents behave like a parent company to order subsidiary. They have a power of life-death over a shop nearby. It does not result from competition between shops.

Third hypothesis is an even distribution of shops like the central place theory. Satsuma-sendai city office made 48 community joint councils in order to build their consensus since the municipal merger, 2003[17] These councils were settled based on an elementary school zone, but on a junior high school zone in inland area. Elementary school began in 1872 as compulsory in Japan. Junior high school was also added to compulsory education in 1947. A school zone of compulsory education was divided by distance from the house of the child going to school from the most far-off place. The distance was determined by law. An elementary school located on the center of a community and its school zone has kept for 148 years and then junior high school zone was determined to get several elementary school zones together and has kept for 73 years. Each school zone has been considered to be an area of the community over the years.

An elementary school zone was settled by distance from a school, then an elementary school located such as even distribution. An elementary school zone matching with community area, the community area coincides with the community joint council area. However, inland areas has been depopulated and some community could not maintain elementary school because of the decrease in number of children. Community in Inland area need to expand its area in order to include more residents for maintaining a function of community. A community area expanded to a junior high school zone, that became a community joint council area. A community joint council area in inland area is based on several junior high school zones, it remains as a property of an elementary school zone that is an even location (See Fig.1 and Fig.2)[18].

Shops nearby should locate on the center of a community for convenience of residents. It seems that shops locate according the central place theory superficially. Residents out of the community never come to a shop. A shop nearby has the clients only from belonging community.

These verification of hypotheses imply that the shops nearby are supported by residents in the area on the purpose to bear the social responsibility in the community. A shop nearby appears under monopolistic competition theory, but under residents' intention. A shop nearby appears to locate on even distribution, but on a center of community. This result makes a shop nearby non-economical business that is a business controlled gently by a community. We found out this fact and include shop nearby into the concept of *community business*. Usually a concept of community business defines as the solution of a regional problem by business so as to make community sustainable[19]. Almost all depopulated and aging communities have no chance to find out the solution by any business. Aged residents want to maintain their own community for as long as they live.. It is a result of maintaining the community from a non-economical conduct. This is a quick-fix solution of depopulated and aged community problems by a business. We would define this fact as a backward-looking style of Community Business.

Industry type are selected by residents such as a barber shop, a beauty shop or an eating house. These types of shops nearby are surviving business in inland communities at last, which provide an essential goods or services for life in the community. Residents think the goods and services are the necessities of life in their community. Someone in the community would continue to purchase goods and services from the shops. It is important for regional development to make a target business which will become a backward-looking one.

Discussion

Our research field is the inland area in Satsuma-sendai city. We changed field to another area and tried to find out backward-looking community business. At first, we researched the island area in Satsuma-sendai city, Koshiki islands in 2013[20]. A center place of a community and a community joint council in the island is each port mostly, where an elementary school and a junior high school were located on. We could not find out a fact such as even distribution of shops. Then, we extracted shops type from a population of the market in a shop nearby. It was classified under the number of an average of the population of the community joint council in the island area, which is 581 in 2013. The type of shop was a barber shop and a beauty shop, or an house eatery. There exited an entry and withdraw of the shop (See Table. 3). There was a similar tendency of shop type between the inland area and the islands area in Satsuma-sendai city.

We research another area in Sou city, which location is 70 kilometers southeast from Satuma-sendai city and a population is 33,669 and the area of the city is 390.11km² in Kagoshima prefecture. Communities in Sou city faced difficulties from depopulated and aged rural society, such as the inland area in Satsuma-dendai city. The main industry in this area has been a cattle industry, especially a swine industry and moved into limelight after the 2011 off the Pacific coast of Tohoku Earthquake. There remains many traces of depopulated and aged society.

We investigated and conjectured the existence of a backward-looking type of community business from the number of entry business (See Table 4.). It seemed to be classified in our target business at Sou city. This type of business was a house-related service, a retailing or a house eatery and restaurant. Consumer behavior of residents in communities in Sou city makes a house-related service remarkable. A farmer prefers to repair his house or cattle shed than to rebuild it, because they never stops in order to take care of his cattle. The cattle industry is one of the main industries in Sou city. House-related services become a necessity for the residents.

House-related service provides a delivered service. A barbershop, a beauty shop or a house eatery provides traveled service. The business of house-related service has an advantage in locating on the place near to residents because of delivered service. The shop nearby is able to put a cheaper price. Then, the residents for house-related service are not pressed on a non-economic behavior and select the shop nearby under economical behavior. We could not call this service business a backward-looking type of community business. There is a possibility for other types of shop, that is a barbershop, a beauty shop or a house eatery and restaurant

We need some consideration from the point of view of regional development or policy. Is the backward-looking type of community business a valid tool for regional development? The residents maintain this business until their life ends. This business makes the community sustainable for several years. It is a result of populated and aged communities in a developed country. We take this tool effectively if the existence of this business is found out in a developing country. This business will be a useful tool for long years until the country developed. In other chapters, *sari-sari* store in Philippine and Bazaar in Tanzania , which are located by residents intendedly, are the good examples which are located by residents intendedly. It is efficient for a developing country to invest in the type of our community business. Then, backward-looking type will change into a forward-looking type.

Conclusion

We defined our shop nearby as a backward-looking type of community business. Their exist-some properties, where it provides a traveled service and it conducts like under the monopolistic competition theory and more it locate on an even distribution like the central place theory. Business continuity is restricted for short years in a developed country and for long years in a developing country.

We often develop a non-economical behavior as a consumer and make a tight relation to a self-employed proprietor. This fact denotes an incomprehensible part of humans over any stage of economic growth

References:

Besser T. L., (2011). The Significance of Community to Business Social Responsibility. Rural Sociology 63(3), 412 -431.

Chamberlin. (1933). Monopolistic Competition, Harvard University Press.

ChristallerW. (1932). Die zentralen Orte in Süddeutschland. Gustav Fischer. Jena.

LëschA. (1940). Die räumliche Ordnung der Wirtschaft. Eine Untersuchung über Standort, Wirtschaftsgebiete und internationalem Handel . Fischer.

Takano, T., (2016). A study on some condition to subsite community business in the depopulated area: An approach of analysis of island area and the inland area Satsukasejdai city. Unpublished doctoral dissertation, Graduate School of Humanities and Social Sciences.

Notes

1. Lewis William presented the theory (Lewis Theory) that the labor force moves from rural to urban as the developing nations grow and industrialize. However, Takano (2016) shows the influx of people from cities associated with the entry and exit of local commercial stores, which is the movement of labor from urban to rural as opposed to Lewis Theory. Rather, it is also the act of urban people moving from urban to rural areas in search of an amenity environment, which can be said to be the reverse Lewis phenomenon. In this joint research, we share this phenomenon as inverse Lewis theory (Nishimura and Hagino 2019).

2. See the following paper. Dacheux É. et Goujion, D. , 2015, "L'économie solidaire : une transition vers une société post capitaliste?, " in Glémain et E. Bioteau eds. Enterprise solidaires:L'économie sociale et solidaire en question(s). Pennes:Press Universitaires de Rennes, pp. 217-232.

3. The 3.11 shock refers to the disruption caused by the Great East Japan Earthquake that occurred on March 11, 2011.

4. There is no fixed definition of Nariwai, but here, in Japan, after the collapse of the bubble economy, while the structure of lifetime employment has collapsed, it refers to a new way of working, such as starting a business in the countryside.

5. Peace Winds Japan (PWJ) is a non-governmental

organization (NGO). PWJ has supported people and communities in 27 countries around the world who have been exposed to natural or humanitarian crises due to natural disasters, conflicts and poverty. In October 2013, PWJ relocated its headquarters from Tokyo to Jinseki Kougen-cho and relocated its representative director, Onishi Kensuke. In addition to taking over the municipal facilities and renewing the experience-based sightseeing facilities, PWJ has set up a "Peace Wanko Japan" project with the aim of zero slaughter of dogs, as well as shelter facilities, dog runs, and hands-on experience facilities that can interact with animals. We protect dogs and cats. Through PWJ's activities, we achieved zero dog and cat slaughter in 2016 in Hiroshima, which was the worst nation in dog and cat slaughter.

6. https://www.britannica.com/topic/bazaar. See also Kojien and Daijisen (Japanese dictionary).

7. Barangay is the smallest autonomic unit in the Philippines. They have a chairperson and an assembly.

8. Sitio is a smaller official unit than Barangay. They are but a zone, not autonomy.

9. As for the cluster 3 (Fig. 6.7), where the barangay hall and two schools exist, we should think that sub-clusters unify with each other continuously and compromise a large cluster.

10. High schools in the Philippines are compulsory. They correspond to junior high schools in Japan.

11. Regional Development Workshop was held by our graduate school member on March, 2019. We visited the inland area in Satsuma-sendai city and Sou-city.

12. This field research made his thesis for a degree. This field study was carried out as a project of Regional Manegement Research Center at our graduate school, and the gained study data are sharing among fellows.

13. Such as [Christaller, 1932], [Lësch, 1940].

14. [Takano, 2016]

15. [Chamberlin]

16. There is a CSR of Community business in a rural area[Besser, 2011] . A self-employed proprietor of the shop will take his CSR plan if he has energy after he finishes his social duties.

17. https://www.city.satsumasendai.lg.jp/www/contents/109 6358500703/index.html

18. Each area of the community joint council is different size because of the population density.

19. Power to Change Trust, https://www.powertochange. org.uk/Community Business NPO, https:// www.communitybusiness.org/

20. [Takano, 2016]